CRIME AND
THE GOTHIC

CRIME AND THE GOTHIC

Identifying the Gothic Footprint in Modern Crime Fiction

Sian MacArthur

For K & D

Published in 2011 by Libri Publishing

Copyright © Sian MacArthur

ISBN 978 1 907471 35 3

Typesetting by Carnegie Publishing Ltd
Cover design by James Hunnisett
Index by james@jalamb.com

Libri Publishing
Brunel House
Volunteer Way
Faringdon
Oxfordshire
SN7 7YR

Tel: +44 (0)845 873 3837

www.libripublishing.co.uk

Cover image: © Ian Sokoliwski

Printed by Ashford Colour Press

Preface

WHEN I was a child, maybe no more than six or seven years old my father took me to Edinburgh Castle. Today, three things from that visit still remain with me; the vastness and height of the beams in the Great Hall, the wonderful simplicity of the stone arch of St. Margaret's Chapel and the gated entrance protecting the gloomy entrance to the Castle's vaults.

It is the memory of those vaults and of the stone steps leading down to them that is the strongest image that I have of that day. It was a part of the Castle that visitors were not permitted to enter freely back then, guided tours were a necessity and so we never actually went down into them, but it is this, I think that began my love affair with all things secretive and dangerous, all things dark, gloomy and that need to remain hidden, all things Gothic.

Fast forward many years and little has changed, only that my interest in the Gothic has moved on from childish fascination with haunted houses and things that go bump in the night. Nevertheless it is this childhood interest that has spurred the writing of this book, a study of the Gothic and the investigation into the ways in which it forms such a fundamental part of one of today's most popular genres, crime fiction.

Kathy Reichs, Patricia Cornwell, Tess Gerritsen, Karin Slaughter, Dan Brown and Mo Hayder are all extremely successful crime fiction writers and each of them regularly top best-seller lists around the world. Of course there are others too, but what has made *these* novelists so successful is the ability of each to offer a slightly different perspective within their writing that brings variation and originality to an increasingly complex genre. Within an over-populated genre such as crime fiction it is only those writers that manage to bring a fresh idea to the table that will make it. Reichs offers an anthropological background, Cornwell a forensic one and Dan Brown has created a religious symbol and icon expert in the form of Professor

Robert Langdon. Gerritsen's investigations often begin in the ER room and Slaughter has re-engaged with the sidekick formula of the earliest detective fiction of Conan-Doyle and Poe in the combination of husband and wife team Sara Linton and Jeff Tolliver. Kate Summerscale has revisited the world of true crime in her whodunit *The Suspicions of Mr Whicher* (interestingly the link between public fascination with crime – 19th-century murder mostly – and the way in which this fascination shapes modern crime fiction is deftly explored in Judith Flanders' *The Invention of Murder*) and finally Stieg Larsson's *Millennium Trilogy* exposes corruption and exploitation through the misadventures of journalist Mikael Blomkvist and his peculiar acquaintance Lisbeth Salander.

In the increasingly difficult quest for originality and a modern, fresh perspective, what has always struck me as unusual is the almost unwavering reliance upon traditional Gothic motif that each of these writers (with rare exception) demonstrate. There is scope to interpret Gerritsen's tales of organ harvest as a modern re-working of Shelley's *Frankenstein* and there is an equally strong argument for reading Dan Brown's stories of mad and corrupt religious authorities as a modern version of Lewis' *The Monk*. Similarly, much of Cornwell's criticism stems from her seeming inability to draw her characters and her plots away from melodramatic Gothic excess.

It is this reliance upon traditional Gothic convention – and the understanding of why such a dynamic modern genre should appear so reliant upon such a seemingly limited and restricted form – that *this* book will explore, offering reasons as to why this is the case with detailed reference and analysis of some of the most up to date crime fiction texts, to explore just how this debt to the Gothic manifests itself in crime writing in the 21st century.

Contents

CHAPTER ONE

Defining the Gothic: Walpole's Benchmark and Later Adaptations

WHEN in 1797 an anonymous author penned an essay entitled 'Terrorist Gothic Writing', those who were subsequently to read the essay and from it form the belief that the Gothic was nothing more than jaunty fun would have been forgiven. Certainly the charming little ditty that appeared within the essay, detailing a proposed recipe for the Gothic, did little to enhance the credibility or the seriousness of this newly emerging genre. Light-weight and jovial in tone, the 'recipe' appeared to have identified the staple ingredients of the genre and seemed to be poking gentle fun at the rigidity and predictability of its conventions:

> *Take* – An old castle, half of it ruinous.
> A long gallery, with a great many doors, some secret ones.
> Three murdered bodies, quite fresh.
> As many skeletons, in chests and presses...
> Mix them, together, in the form of three volumes, to be taken at any
> of the watering-places before going to bed.[1]

Whilst this 'recipe' did indeed identify many of the stylistic tendencies of the Gothic genre and acknowledge the often repetitive features of its plots, what it failed to do was to give any indication as to the potentially greater significance of those Gothic texts that adhered so rigidly to the strict 'rules' of the genre. It had found the skeletons in the cupboard, so to speak, but it had not identified them.

Readers of this anonymous essay therefore would indeed have been forgiven for interpreting this light-weight analysis as indicative of a light-weight genre; that it was something frivolous and not to be taken seriously.

Yes, they would have been forgiven, but they would have been mistaken too; the mistake being that such an assumption would have been a gross under-estimation of not only what the Gothic genre was, but also how significant a form of writing it was to become over the next several hundred years.

There is after all no escaping the importance of the 'Gothic' as a move-ment that has dramatically shaped many forms of art over a very long period of time. One of the 'most influential artistic styles and artistic genres of the last four centuries'[2], Gothic trace is evident in architecture, music and media spanning a far greater period of time than any other genre. Modern box office successes such as the Harry Potter films, the Twilight trilogy and Dan Brown's *The Da Vinci Code* and *Angels and Demons* are each examples of the way in which the Gothic manages to manifest itself in the world of 21st-century cinema. *True Blood*, *Bedlam* and even *Most Haunted* reflect the insatiable thirst of television audiences for Gothic-influenced drama and reality TV, and equally the influence of the Gothic upon modern literature in particular is an aspect that simply cannot be ignored. Indeed the extent to which the Gothic has had (and continues to have) such a significant influence upon so many different genres of writing has led to the recogni-tion that many authors have 'derive[d] their techniques of suspense and their sense of the archaic directly from the original Gothic fiction.'[3]

As a movement the 'Gothic' in its most original or 'pure' state is very much homogeneous in form, but despite its tight restrictions and limited boundaries it remains hugely influential. The way in which the Gothic has, over many years, continued to dominate the narrative direction and stylistic focus of so many different genres of literature is something that is particu-larly interesting, and the focus of this book will be to explore this early Gothic and the influence that it has had on shaping one of the most popular and enduring genres – that of crime fiction.

It will explore the development of detective fiction as a logical extension of the Gothic, and seek to explain fully how these two genres (the Gothic and Gothic-influenced detective fiction) are essentially responsible for the existence of modern crime fiction, and it will determine how writers such as Robert Bloch, Ian Rankin, Thomas Harris, Patricia Cornwell and Mo Hayder have each been influenced by the Gothic form and the ways in which this influence manifests itself in their work.

It would seem appropriate therefore, to take a moment to fully explore what we mean by the term 'Gothic' in relation to those early Gothic works and subsequent key Gothic novels that set the bar so specifically as to exactly what the term entails. Whilst it is true that the Gothic has enjoyed many flourishes, adaptations and changes in form over the last few hundred years, to study it in its purist form, that which will be identified and referred to as first phase Gothic will ultimately expose what in itself the Gothic truly is. It will also offer explanations into why, in recent years, the genre has become such a significant part of that which we now identify as crime fiction.

How then to offer a definition of 'Gothic' in this book concisely and accurately? A difficult task to undertake, and yet one that is necessary if the claims of this book are to be fully realised. At its most basic the Gothic can be defined as that which combines desire and suffering in such a fashion as to induce feelings of fear for one or more of the characters within the text and generate suspense for the reader in response to that character's (or those characters') fear. In order to understand the concept of the 'Gothic' fully, particularly the way in which desire and suffering are seen to be linked, it is essential to explore in the first instance the origins of the genre and identify those texts that are largely accepted as being the first Gothic novels. By looking collectively at early Gothic texts in this way, a set of clear conventions should become apparent upon which such definitions, recognitions and expectations of the Gothic genre may be balanced.

Early Gothic Form — Horace Walpole and Clara Reeve

When, then did the Gothic as an identifiable genre emerge? And over what given period does this first phase of Gothic take place? It is widely accepted that Horace Walpole's *The Castle of Otranto* (1764) is indeed the first Gothic novel. Although Walpole's effort appears somewhat ludicrous and far-fetched by today's modern standards, it was nevertheless well received by the readers of its day. Because of this it has certainly earned its place within the canon of significant British texts as being that which effectively created a new form of literature and established a clearly identifiable set of conventions which for the most part are still a distinct part of both Gothic and crime writing today.

That said it would be erroneous to credit Walpole with creating an entirely new genre himself. Gothic themes had after all been present in literature long before Walpole put pen to paper. The mid-18th-century poetry of Edward Young, Robert Blair, Thomas Parnell, Henry Kirke and Thomas Gray to name a few is enough to show that certainly by the time Walpole was writing, Gothic *sentiment* was indeed well established. Consider the following extract from Thomas Gray's *Elegy Written in a Country Churchyard* (1751):

Now fades the glimmering landscape on the sight,
And all the air a solemn stillness holds,
Save where the beetle wheels his droning flight,
And drowsy tinklings lull the distant folds:

Save that from yonder ivy-mantled tower
The moping owl does to the moon complain
Of such as, wandering near her secret bower,
Molest her ancient solitary reign.

Beneath those rugged elms, that yew-tree's shade,
Where heaves the turf in many a mouldering heap,
Each in his narrow cell for ever laid,
The rude Forefathers of the hamlet sleep.[4]

Effectively what Walpole adopted was a new structure, that of the novel, in which to suitably and appropriately *house* this sentiment. By capturing the mood of the Graveyard Poets, and by developing the form of the *story* itself, Walpole hit upon a much more successful format for the genre and, perhaps unintentionally, sketched out the blueprint from which it would rapidly develop.

Let us then turn our attention to this great forerunner of all things Gothic for a moment and take a look at the novel as a whole before taking it apart and identifying those aspects of the text that we now take for granted as being the building blocks of the Gothic. In the first instance, this fictional novel presents itself as being a long lost historical document originating from Naples in the year 1529, and claims to relay a peculiar (and supposedly genuine) sequence of events that are assumed to have taken place somewhere between 1095 at the earliest and 1243 at the latest.

It is, in its essence, a tale of lineage and that of a father's mad quest to beget himself a son and heir so that his ancestral line may continue. It is set, as its title suggests within a castle and this castle is fashioned with a huge and complicated network of underground tunnels and vaults which form a crucial part of the texts for two reasons. The first of these is purely functional and linked to the main plot of the text in that they offer a physical means of escape from Manfred for the fleeing virgin Isabella. As she is forced to travel through these tunnels a greater sense of suspense and fear can be generated for the reader, and in this respect we hit upon the most fundamental aspect of the Gothic as mentioned earlier, that is the link between the *desire* and *suffering* that is created once the villain (Manfred in this example) has set his sights on attaining that which is not freely or readily available to him (Isabella).

4

The second way in which the tunnels hold importance is their meta-phorical significance as a personification of the dark and twisted mind of Manfred himself. This aspect links to the sub-text of the plot, exposing as it does the tyrannous mindset of the villain of the text. This presence of both main and sub plot within the text is evidence of the leap forward that the Gothic was able to make once its structure had been revised: there simply was no scope within the Graveyard poetry to accommodate such a leap in the complexity of the narrative.

The characters that we find within the text are also deliberately crafted, and these stock character types remain very much a staple feature of later Gothic texts. In Isabella we have the victim; a beautiful virgin marginalised and hunted down by the abhorrent demands of a patriarchal society. Ironically her beauty and her virginity become less of an asset and more of a curse as they draw to her Manfred who demonstrates overwhelming mascu-line rage, uncontrollable sexual urges and impulses and who is quick to set aside his weak, passive and effectively impotent wife, Hippolita, in pursuit of the spirited yet seemingly doomed Isabella. Such is the importance of ancestral lineage that Manfred becomes determined to beget himself a new heir at any cost, and much of the text's pace and suspense is generated and maintained as Manfred attempts to hunt Isabella down and catch her as she flees through the vast underbelly of the castle itself.

In this respect Manfred becomes the active aggressor within the plot and by far the most interesting character in the tale. Demonisation of this sort was a character trait and stylistic feature that would very quickly become the norm for Gothic writing, and subsequent Gothic villains were often constructed in this way for the purpose of making them suitably 'attractive' for the reader. Consequently the villain becomes 'the most complex and interesting character in Gothic fiction', a character who is 'awe-inspiring, endlessly resourceful in pursuit of his often opaquely evil ends, and yet possessed of a mysterious attractiveness' and one who 'stalks from the pages of one Gothic novel to another, manipulating the doom of others...'[5]

Evidently this is true of Manfred, the villain of the tale and a symbol of tyrannical masculinity that is a truly terrifying representation of patriarchal society. Manfred's desire is finally quashed at the end of the narrative by the heroic intervention of young Theodore, a veritable angel to Manfred's demon, and who it transpires, in a remarkable and uncanny twist of fate (notwithstanding the important role of Providence), is revealed to be the true heir to the Castle of Otranto. In an unmistakeable moral message that evil will not prosper, Manfred is forced to forfeit all claims to the castle, and has to be stopped at the end of the tale from being overcome by despondency and using his dagger to 'dispatch himself.'[6]

The Castle of Otranto is also largely credited with initiating the trend for inclusion of a mysterious past or history within the narrative that can relate to either the characters themselves or relate more directly to the way in which the plot unfolds. Secrets such as these are often hidden in ancient manuscripts or, as is the case in this example, riddled within a seemingly bizarre and meaningless prophecy. Dreams also are a relative mainstay of the Gothic and, although not a part of Walpole's novel, they usually appear at critical moments when the dreamer is under the most pressure or stress, bringing with them messages and deeper meanings that are often directly related to the whatever central mystery drives the main plot. The supernatural too, has always had a strong role to play within traditional or first phase Gothic texts. Certainly it is something that features heavily in *The Castle of Otranto*: consider the rather peculiar behaviour of the helmet that kills poor Conrad and the somewhat eerie ghostly movement of the portrait of the Grandfather.

Whilst it is important to recognise each of these themes within Walpole's text it is equally important to acknowledge the way in which they each quickly became staple 'ingredients' of the Gothic as more and more texts, each in a similar vein were written. In 1777 Clara Reeve produced *The Old English Baron* (originally titled *The Champion of Virtue, a Gothic Tale*), probably the most credible and certainly the most well known follow up to Walpole's *Otranto*. Almost immediately after this, in the years up to 1800, a Gothic boom developed where writers such as Matthew Lewis, Ann Radcliffe, Sophia Lee, William Beckford and many others all produced a mass of texts which we have now come to recognise as early, or first phase Gothic.

Indeed there is no mistaking these early Gothic texts, so specific are the conventions that they adhere to, and Reeve's *The Old English Baron* (1777) demonstrates exactly how the genre was beginning to take shape. The similarities to Walpole's *The Castle of Otranto* are many, and the book itself was born from Walpole's effort, as Reeve herself points out in her preface to the third edition of the text (1780) by stating that her novel 'is the literary offspring of the *Castle of Otranto*, written upon the same plan.'[7]

The story itself centres on the aristocratic family residing at the castle of Lovel, the mysterious demise of the first Lord Lovel, and the subsequent discovery of the missing natural heir to the estate, Edmund, the supposed son of a local peasant. It features the supernatural in the form of dreams and mysterious apparitions in a similar effort to *Otranto*, and likewise the sense of mania that pervades both novels is abated when order is restored at the end of the novel and Providence intervenes to ensure that only the good prosper and that heritage and lineage are once again proved to be pure.

As with *Otranto*, the central preoccupation in *The Old English Baron* is the lawful and proper restoration of the Castle of Lovel to its rightful owner. Throughout the course of the narrative it comes to light that in an attempt to usurp the rightful owner of the Castle (Lord Lovel himself, Edmund's father), Walter Lovel (kinsman to Lord Lovel) arranged for the Lord to be murdered and subsequently tried to marry his widow so that he might assume ownership of the Castle and its estate. In an attempt to hide the evidence of the murder, Walter Lovel proceeded to bury the corpse under a closet within the disused East Wing, and it is only when Edmund himself spends a night within the apartment that ghostly goings on are revealed and the true awfulness of what has occurred is brought to light:

> The first thing that presented itself to their view was a complete suit of armour that seemed to have fallen down on an heap. "Behold" said Edmund. "This made the noise we heard above." They took it up, and examined it piece by piece; the inside of the breast-plate was stained with blood. "See here!" said Edmund; "what do you think of this?"
>
> "'Tis my lord's armour," said Joseph; "I know it well. Here has been bloody work in this closet!"[8]

Like Walpole, Reeve manages to obtain distance from the present within her novel by presenting it as an old manuscript upon which the story of the family is recorded. Arguably both Walpole and Reeve can be considered as forerunners of developing the Gothic tendency to generate distance between the actual context that they are written in and the period in history that they purport to have taken place in. Certainly this narrative technique was a trend adopted by many later Gothic writers, and we will be able to see to what effect and purpose this tendency has when we look to examples of Gothic writing by Lewis and Radcliffe.

The Old English Baron also carries character types that are in many ways similarly constructed to Walpole's characters. Walter Lovel, like Manfred before him, becomes the villain within the plot. His atrocities against Lord Lovel and his wife are gradually revealed throughout the duration of the narrative, and like Manfred, Walter eventually has to formally hand back all rights to the Castle. Walter then retreats from England and enters into the service of the Greek Emperor of the time (Manfred is equally subject to a life of retreat as he joins a convent and engages one would hope in atonement for those he has wronged).

There are also interesting parallels to draw between the two heroes of the texts, Theodore and Edmund, in the way that each of these characters manages to bear up against the series of wrongs done to them throughout the course of the novels. Theodore falls victim to Manfred's rage, and is at one point sentenced to death for his seeming audacity towards him. Likewise Edmund is constantly undermined by the jealous natures of his 'siblings', the blood children of his benefactor Lord Baron Fitz-Owen. That both of these men bear these injustices with such patience and seeming good grace is paramount to the overriding moral of the Gothic that evil will not prosper and that ultimately the good and the true will out.

Although Reeve's novel differs in that it is significantly less sensational than Walpole's (it is certainly presented under the guise of being more historically authentic), in terms of ticking features off of the 'Gothic checklist', its similarities to its predecessor are numerous. It would appear that whilst Walpole created something arguably original in form (the novel format in which to accommodate this new breed of Gothic writing specifically), much of the popular fiction crafted over the next few decades would do nothing more than offer imitative and frequently inferior clones of this very successful novel.

Certainly the strict stylistic conventions of the Gothic have been studied extensively and written about numerous times. Whether referred to as 'staple Gothic ingredients'[9] or 'key characteristics'[10] of the genre, what each of these studies do is to reflect the same thing; and that is that the 'consistency of the genre'[11] is dependent upon recurrent application of each of these conventions:

> When thinking of the Gothic novel, a set of characteristics springs readily to mind: an emphasis on portraying the terrifying, a common insistence on archaic settings, a prominent use of the supernatural, the presence of highly stereotyped characters and the attempt to deploy and perfect techniques of literary suspense are the most significant. Used in this sense, 'Gothic' fiction is the fiction of the haunted castle, of heroines preyed upon by unspeakable terrors, of the blackly lowering villain, of ghosts, vampires, monsters and werewolves.[12]

Indeed, it would seem to appear that the stylistic tendencies of uncapped madness, sensationalism and melodrama in the Gothic genre generated amusement for several writers between 1800 and 1820 and during this time a number of Gothic parodies and satires emerged, each with a risible tone aimed at exploiting Gothic convention for the sake of humour. Perhaps the most famous of all of these is Jane Austen's gently satirical *Northanger Abbey* (1817), in which the young Catherine Morland, unlikely heroine and avid reader of Gothic fiction, finds herself invited to stay at the mysterious Northanger Abbey. Overwhelmed by the prospect and with her mind completely saturated with Gothic wonder, Catherine finds mystery in everything she comes across, crediting even the most ordinary object with Gothic significance. Perhaps the most pertinent example of this Gothic 'flight of fancy' occurs upon Catherine's arrival at her apartment within the Abbey and her notice of a rather intriguing chest located to one side of the fireplace:

> This is strange indeed! I did not expect such a sight as this! – An
> immense heavy chest! – What can it hold? Why should it be placed here?
> – Pushed back too, as if meant to be out of sight! I will look into it – cost
> me what it may, I will look into it...'[13]

Without doubt Catherine's acute interest in the chest is indicative of her swooning fancy and a temperament induced by the Gothic novels that she has been reading, and one can only imagine her disappointment when the chest is revealed to harbour nothing more sinister than a white cotton bed quilt.

Although by no means a scathing attack upon the genre, Austen's novel can certainly be interpreted as being written by one who is perhaps a little exasperated and a touch amused by the repetitive nature and rigidity displayed by these early first phase Gothic texts. Evidently Austen was not alone in these sentiments, and the years between 1810 and 1820 saw many writers producing novels of similar outlook. Easton Stannard Barrett's *The Heroine* (1813) and Thomas Love Peacock's *Nightmare Abbey* (1818) are probably, after *Northanger Abbey*, the best examples of early Gothic parody for those wishing to explore this issue further.

Revolutionary Misgivings in the Work of Matthew Lewis and Ann Radcliffe

Having identified the scope for satire and parody within the Gothic, it would be doing the genre a disservice if we were to group each of the Gothic texts produced within this period under the umbrella of unoriginal plagiarism.

Evidently there are a number of writers who flourished under the rules and regulations of the Gothic and managed to work individually within its conventions. Indeed it can be argued that within such tight formulaic constraints, even larger scope for personal input was created.

For Matthew Lewis and Ann Radcliffe, the formulaic nature of the Gothic form became in itself an opportunity by which both writers could make subtle social and political observations under the mask of Gothic excess and sensationalism. It would appear that by writing within a genre that lacked a degree of credibility and that was considered relatively 'low brow', pertinent and relevant observations could be made without the author needing to put his or her neck on the line so to speak.

The concept of a link between the Gothic novel and, in particular, the French Revolution is a subject that has also been written about extensively, with the recurrent claim that novels of this period cannot be read independently of their political and social contexts and that rather, they must be read as 'the product of [their] revolutionary commotion.'[14] Certainly there is strong evidence to link the increasing popularity of the Gothic during the years in which the French Revolution took place and the Revolution itself, with the general consensus being that this was for the most part due 'to the widespread anxieties and fears in Europe aroused by the turmoil in France finding a kind of horror or catharsis in tales of darkness, confusion, blood and terror.'[15]

Certainly the Gothic texts produced during this period, of which those by Lewis and Radcliffe are the most well known, are radically different in tone to the earlier Gothic writings of Walpole and Reeve. Considerably darker in tone with much greater emphasis on bloody violence and overt sexual references there is indeed a strong argument for the drawing of significant parallels between the turmoil of the French Revolution and the turmoil inherent in the texts of the period. Writing in 1800 the Marquis de Sade recognised the opportunity for writers producing works of Gothic fiction to inject cultural context both metaphorically and allegorically into their work, explaining that alongside the upheaval of the French Revolution old-fashioned novels simply paled into insignificance and in order to inject suspense and to compete with the sheer awfulness of Revolutionary battle it became necessary to 'call upon the aid of hell itself'[16].

Working within the tight conventions of the genre, writers such as Radcliffe and Lewis were able to infuse degrees of anxiety into their texts that were specifically related to the cultural context of the period. Perhaps, ironically, greater scope for personal observations and commentaries was generated as a direct result of the very tightness of the Gothic structure;

certainly metaphorical writing allowed for a greater degree of anonymity on the part of the author and generated distance from political ramification.

In order to explore this concept further, let us look to specific examples from each of these two writers, and assess the ways in which they seem to not only reflect, but bear direct relevance to the political context in which they were written (that is the French Revolution of 1789–99). Although essentially an event that forms part of French history, the Revolution and the huge political upheaval that it caused did not go unnoticed this side of the English Channel, and there was perhaps vested British interest in the Revolution as a result of the overthrow of the monarchy during their Civil War of the previous century. By the time revolution broke out in France, British monarchy had long been restored with the recall of Charles II to England in 1660, but following the uncertainty and anxiety of this partic-ular period keen political eyes would have watched very carefully the events as they unfolded across the channel.

Indeed the years between 1789 and 1799 saw very many commentaries written in response to the events taking place in France at that time. As you would expect, opinion was divided for or against the Revolution. Thomas Paine's *Rights of Man* (1791) for example, was largely in favour of the senti-ment and driving force (although perhaps not the levels of violence produced) behind the movement. On the other hand, there was as much written that spoke out against the Revolution and the one most pertinent to this study is Edmund Burke's *Reflections on the Revolution in France* (1790).

What is particularly interesting in this particular example of anti-Revolution writing is the Gothic imagery that Burke uses to attempt to give meaning to, ratify and define the events unfolding in France that he does not comprehend (in that they are alien to the way in which he believes the country should be structured) and that consequentially he is frightened of.

His writing is characterised by images of fear; with the suggestion of criminals and felons lurking in the shadows threatening to overturn nobility and gentility without as much as a second thought. It is also highly dramatic in terms of the show of emotion displayed by Burke, and in this respect is reminiscent of Gothic writing. If we consider Burke's assessment of the Revolution in France as the 'grand ingredient in the cauldron'[17] of unspeakable wickedness we can begin to understand how Burke is adopting the language and imagery of the Gothic to convey his fear. In Gothic style, Burke is able to personify the revolution itself, asking if he is to:

...seriously facilitate a madman, who has escaped from the protecting restraint and wholesome darkness of his cell, on restoration to the enjoyment of light and liberty? Am I to congratulate the highwayman and murderer who has broken prison upon the recovery of his natural rights?[18]

Obviously it is human nature to want to give face to and to attempt to quantify the unknown, but that Burke so consistently employs Gothic imagery to stress his point and to strengthen his argument demonstrates the significance of the Gothic as a form of writing at that time. He continually refers to the Revolution as 'monstrous'[19] and his writing is driven by passion and sensationalism that are themselves very typical of the style.

What this also demonstrates is the way in which the Gothic style can be readily incorporated into other forms of writing to express more effectively the range of emotions experienced in response to a specific event or events, and in light of this we can perhaps begin to understand why the Gothic is such a strong presence within crime fiction. With this in mind then, is there scope for reading Lewis' *The Monk* (1796) and Radcliffe's *The Italian* (1797) as more than simple, singularly dimensional Gothic novels? That there is clear and distinct correlation between the Gothic novel and the French Revolution is certainly an interesting perspective, and it is largely accepted that Gothic novels of this period are indeed 'the inevitable result of the revolutionary shocks which all of Europe had suffered.'[20]

Certainly the notion of a deeper subtext within *The Monk* is not a new idea and there is a significant critical appreciation that recognises the proportion of the subtext that leans towards 'the discovery of the infinite danger within or beneath what had seemed familiar and safe.'[21] Notwithstanding the numerous 'safe havens' within the text that are subsequently revealed to be anything but safe (the differing representations of the Capuchin Cathedral in the opening chapter, or the murderous revelations surrounding the St Clare Convent, for example), there is a general feeling of undermining and threat of collapse of established orders that runs prevalently within the text. It is in light of this ongoing theme of collapsing orders that alternative meaning may be derived from Lewis' work.

Perhaps the most significant example of the deeper meaning and significance present within *The Monk* is the destruction of the St Clare Convent, and numerous attempts have been made to link this event as absolutely representative of specific events occurring in France at the time. It has been suggested that this particular episode is meant to represent the September Massacres of 1792 and also that it could bear distinct relation to the fall of the Bastille in 1789. Whilst there is no proof that either of these interpretations, or indeed any other similar interpretation is in anyway accurate, it would be foolhardy not to consider the possibility that *The Monk* is very much a product of its cultural environment, or that the events of the Revolution do not have at the very least *some* influence upon the direction and meaning of the text.

Lewis' text is also significant in terms of the developing role of the villain in the Gothic genre, and this increased complexity of character is something that simply was not present in the earlier texts by Walpole and Reeve. Certainly Lewis' contribution to the development of the representation of the 'villain' within the text highlights the capacity for the Gothic to be more than a simple ghost story, and this is absolutely evident in the way in which Ambrosio's 'splendid potential is twisted and defeated by destructive conflicting qualities.'[22] That Ambrosio possess this degree of both good *and* evil undoubtedly makes for a more interesting and perplexing character and is of course a step forward from the singular dimension of evil present within the villains of earlier Gothic work. To this extent 'the Monk is distinguishable from such earlier figures as Walpole's Manfred and Ann Radcliffe's Montoni by the extent to which explicitly described social influences are implicated in the perversion of his abilities.'[23] The Monk is also very different from the villain in one of Lewis' other texts – the much shorter novel *Mistrust*. Of course *Mistrust* did not appear until 1808, some years after *The Monk* was published, and when it did appear, it did so within a collection of much shorter stories grouped under the title *Romantic Tales*. Significantly less barbaric, less violent and much less of a whirlwind in pace, Lewis' tale has all the trappings of the Gothic (patriarchal fathers, secrets, crypts and infanticide) in the same way that *The Monk* did, but it has none of the fervour and brutality of its predecessor. Whilst *Mistrust's* Rudiger is indeed a Gothic villain of some note, he is comparatively small fry to the behaviour of and atrocities performed by *The Monk's* Ambrosio.

What Lewis has been shown to have done with the role of villain within *The Monk* is indeed an interesting development. Whereas the motivations of both Manfred and Walter Lovel of Reeve's *The Old English Baron* are relatively simple to understand, the psychology of the Monk is significantly more complex. This notion of one being simultaneously good *and* evil, or hero *and* victim, is something that we shall see again to great effect in Mary Shelley's *Frankenstein*, and is also evident in Stevenson's *Jekyll and Hyde*, Maturin's *Melmoth* and Godwin's *Caleb Williams*. It is also a frequently recurring theme that has found a suitable and willing host within much modern crime fiction – in the work of Thomas Harris and Patricia Cornwell in particular.

There is also great change in the construction of the female characters within Lewis' text. On the one hand there is Antonia who in many ways represents a typical Gothic heroine. Marginalised and hunted down by Ambrosio she attempts to reclaim power and find escape for herself from the lust-driven Monk, but in the end proves no match for his malicious intent and, in a move that denotes a dramatic step forward in the degree of violence and aggression within the Gothic plot, her rape and murder ensue.

The other dominant female character is of course Matilda, sent direct from Satan in female form to bring about Ambrosio's ruin and sadistic death. Of course Matilda is not *entirely* responsible for Ambrosio's destruction, waking as she does emotions and desires that have up until this point remained dormant within the arrogant and egotistical Monk. The point is that even within the most wholesome and well meaning of characters (particularly *male* characters) there is always the capacity for evil, a latent darker side that needs often only a little persuasion to cease its dormancy. The message here is strong and carries with it a distinct Revolutionary message; that things are not always as they seem and that there may very well be underhand forces at work whose sole intention is to cause or at the very least *encourage* ruination and destruction. There is also a clear warning present within the text – that having trust and faith will in no way guarantee safety if that trust and faith is placed in the hands of those will not respect it.

To some extent the same can be said of *The Italian*; that there is indeed a strong whiff of the Revolution evident in its subtext and there is evidence to suggest that Radcliffe, like many of her contemporaries 'situate[d] their novels at a discreet distance (spatially and/or temporarily) from current events while at the same time commenting upon political and familial questions sparked by the Revolutionary decade.'[24] Evidently this is true, and Radcliffe, like Lewis, has indeed opted to site her novel outside of the realms of the political upheaval in France and away from the inevitable fallout from the Revolution as felt in England. She sets *The Italian* in Naples in the year 1758 (Lewis' *The Monk* is set in Spain, but at an unspecified date) and thus generates a satisfactory distance from her cultural surroundings to enable her novel to address those areas of conflict and turmoil that she sees happening around her with suitable anonymity.

It is also possible to interpret this remote setting as directly reflecting another social conflict happening at the time, this being the fallout from the clash between 'representatives of the feudal past' (Schedoni and the Marchesa) and 'representatives of the dawning modern era'[25] (Ellena and Vivaldi). Whilst there is some degree of truth to be found in the concept of a battle between old and new being the driving force behind the Revolution itself, for the theme within the novel to be read as occurring as a direct response to the Revolution, then one would have to assume that it did not feature in any Gothic novel that appeared before the Revolution began. A swift look back to Walpole's *Otranto* is enough to prove that this is not the case at all; Isabella is just as feisty a heroine as Ellena, representative along with Theodore and Edmund of the *promise* and the *optimism* of the modern age, and just as capable of rebelling against her oppressor as Ellena is. Nevertheless, *The Italian* should not be read out of context; there quite simply is too much tyranny, too much oppression and such a strong sense of rebellion within it that it is impossible not to credit it with at least some degree of political savvy.

Like Lewis, Radcliffe has also chosen to steer the Gothic into new territory whereby supposed safe havens and seeming respected figures of authority are deeply flawed and capable of committing the most heinous crimes. Both men *and* women are shown to possess ambiguous morality, capable of following and pursuing those darker desires that will cause the suffering and, certainly in the case of *The Monk's* Antonia, the annihilation of others. Schedoni, whilst a figure of public admiration, reveals himself to be capable of subterfuge and scheming; a conspirator who whilst in the act of plotting becomes 'most startlingly alive'[26] and the Marchesa, despite her public demeanour revels in the very slyness of the cunning she engages in.

Another significant change to novels of this period is the absence of the clear-cut role of hero, specifically the faith held by the hero that Providence will intervene to ensure that there are positive outcomes and that the villain(s) will suffer the fate that they deserve. By the time Lewis and Radcliffe were writing the emphasis had very much shifted away from mere good luck and the unshakeable belief that things will just work out and the good will prosper just by *being* good. In these later texts it seems that you very much contribute to your own fate and are to a certain extent responsible for your own future. Therefore it is essential that Vivaldi not only survives the Inquisition that he faces; he needs to prove himself against the horrors that he is subjected to. That this particular Gothic boundary has shifted so dramatically in these texts is interesting and one wonders whether such changes would have occurred had these particular novels been written at a time of less cultural upheaval.

Humanity Under Threat — The Representation of the 'Monster' in the Work of Mary Shelley and John Polidori

The way in which the boundaries of the Gothic were beginning to be pushed and changes made to the predictable nature of the genre can be seen with great effect in Mary Shelley's *Frankenstein*. Written during the onset of the Industrial Revolution it is essentially a Gothic tale in which the main drive behind the narrative is one man's ill-placed desire to create human life. In this respect Shelley's novel bears resemblance to the earliest Gothic text by Walpole whose villain Manfred was similarly consumed by the desire to generate life. Of course the motivations and the manner in which this 'life' was to be generated differ significantly between the texts, but the link between the *desire* for life and the *suffering* that it causes are much alike and gives Shelley's tale its strongest Gothic link.

First published in 1818, the novel in its written form is the result of a horror story told by Shelley one evening during a vacation at Byron's Villa Diodati. As means of entertainment, each of the guests (including Byron himself, Polidori and Percy Shelley) would compete against each other telling ghost or horror stories, and it is out of this meeting of experimental and wonderfully dark imaginations that the novel was born. Interestingly despite its obvious links to the Gothic genre, Shelley's novel is also very much a product of the Romantic period in which it was conceived; the vision of the monster left alone to wander the landscapes of Europe to contemplate his utter misery whilst taking in the wonder of the natural world carries with it a very real and definite sense of Romanticism as the monster finds himself inflicted with the Romantic condition of simultaneous misery and inspiration:

> It was dark when I awoke; I felt cold also, and half frightened, as it were, instinctively, finding myself so desolate...I was a poor, helpless, miserable wretch...I sat down and wept.

> Soon a gentle light stole over the heavens, and gave me a sensation of pleasure. I started up and beheld a radiant form rise from among the trees. I gazed with a kind of wonder.[27]

Frankenstein also carries with it the first strands of science fiction within its main plot, and this scientific aspect represents a completely new direction for the Gothic, which is the complete removal of any supernatural connotation within the narrative. (This is perhaps not all that surprising given that Mary was of course the offspring of the very rationally and practically minded Mary Wollstonecraft and William Godwin.) It is not the only of Shelley's Romantic Gothic tales to do so – her much shorter text *The Heir of Mondolfo*, despite clinging onto much that is traditionally Gothic (the castle and the obsession with producing an appropriate heir) shuns many of the other traditional trappings of the Gothic (the supernatural for example) in favour of ominous weather and similar omens of doom and despair.

Whereas the theme of the supernatural had been present in a number of Gothic texts, there is ultimately and absolutely nothing supernatural about the existence of the monster *Frankenstein*; he is very much a human (Victor Frankenstein's) creation and that he is man-made as such completely abates the need for a supernatural explanation or presence within the text. Superhuman in terms of his physical strength he may be, but definitely not supernatural. This scientific aspect to the text, particularly the 'highly *abstracted* creative powers'[28] of Victor Frankenstein although making for a fantastically terrifying read may also have cultural significance, in that when given suitable 'scientific context'[29] (that of the Industrial Revolution perhaps) they contribute to the novel's main theme, this being 'the aspiration of modern masculinist scientists to be technically creative divinities.'[30] Certainly it is possible that without the scientific context and influence of the Industrial Revolution Shelley might well have written a text in which the themes, events and outcome were very different.

As well as this interest in the scientific and the biologically experimental, another significant difference between *Frankenstein* and its precursors is the almost complete absence of any 'hero' within the story. Although a great many of the other typical Gothic characters are present within the text (villain and victim(s) specifically), the text is markedly different from not only its predecessors but also a great many of its contemporaries by the notable absence of a hero, or at the least a would-be hero. Indeed the closest we come to an example of heroism is the monster's declaration at the very end of the novel that 'the bitter sting of remorse will not seek to rankle in [his] wounds until death shall close them for ever'[31] as he vows to bring about his own death by ascending his 'funeral pile triumphantly, and exult[ing] in the agony of the torturing flames.'[32]

Of course that he desires and evidently feels that he deserves such a horrific and lonely death serve only to remind us that he is, of course, just as much villain as he is victim and here Shelley is quite clearly developing the trend initiated by Radcliffe and Lewis to substantiate characters and make them less easily definable. Ostensibly throughout the novel Shelley presses upon the reader that the monster's responsibility for his actions is negligible – owing perhaps to the truly awful way that he has been excluded from society based solely upon his hideous appearance – and as a result of this we have possibly the strongest example ever written of proving that it is nurture not nature that ultimately determines character.

There is however another villain in the piece who we must not ignore, and that is Victor Frankenstein himself. Whether his true villainy lies in the creation of the monster or the manner in which he shunned it once it was brought to life is an interesting topic for debate, but whichever side of the fence you sit on there is no escaping the fact that Victor Frankenstein is an awful representation of humanity who ultimately pays the price for meddling in things that man has no right to interfere with. True to traditional Gothic sentiment, and very much in keeping with the definition of the Gothic that was outlined at the opening of this chapter, it is Frankenstein's *desires* that are the root cause of all of the *suffering* (of which there is a great deal) within the text and that above all else seals his place as the ultimate villain of the piece.

It is this absence of a hero that prevents the tale from having any degree of satisfactory conclusion, and in this respect *Frankenstein* also differs from its Gothic predecessors. With Frankenstein dead and the monster drifting off to his death on an ice-raft at the end of the text there was the option, had Shelley so wished, to give her tale some sense of optimism or positivity in its conclusion, instead we have this:

> He sprung from the cabin window, as he said this, upon the ice-raft
> which lay close to the vessel. He was soon borne away by the waves, and
> lost in darkness and distance.[33]

That there is no such restoration of order and new found happiness at the end of the text, as we have come to expect from the Gothic, is significant. Quite simply we are not supposed to rest easy once we have finished reading; simply not allowed to plod along just as we did before. Ultimately there is a deep sense of warning and of danger within Shelley's subtext, and it revolves entirely around the arrogance and blindsightedness of man. That there is such a strong sense of cultural anxiety and a distinct warning as to the potential dangers of ill-conceived scientific experimentation should not be ignored, but by the same measure to read too heavily into it would be to misinterpret my meaning here. Certainly *Frankenstein* and a great many other Gothic texts can be understood to be offering a degree of cultural commentary, but this in no way means that they are necessarily *driven* to make such an offering.

Both arrogance and blindness do however have a large part to play in another significant Gothic tale from this period, and that is John Polidori's *The Vampyre*. First published in New Monthly Magazine in 1819, it appeared in print only a year after the first edition of Shelley's *Frankenstein* was printed and depicts yet another massive change in direction for the Gothic novel. Widely regarded as being the first vampire novel to be written in the English language it takes its inspiration from the myths, folklores and travellers' tales that had for very many years captured the imaginations of the peasant classes in the Balkan regions of South-East Europe. This European influence is given new direction and perspective as Polidori sets his tale within the aristocratic elite of London society, and there is deliberate irony evident in the outward aristocratic appearance of the villain of the piece, Lord Ruthven, that masks the sub-human impulses and barbaric behaviour of which he is shown to be capable. Like Shelley's novel there is a distinct sense of *warning* present in Polidori's tale and this sentiment is evident in both the main text (Aubrey's desperate attempt to try and prevent his sister's marriage to Lord Ruthven) and also in the sub-text (Polidori's suggestion that there is something to be feared in the rakish, libertine behaviour and seeming freedom of the powerful upper classes). Aubrey's sister's refusal to heed the warning of course results in her death and, just as in *Frankenstein* there is absolutely no sense of resolution at the end of the text, as we assume that Lord Ruthven has escaped and is free to pursue his pleasure as he chooses. Certainly the admonitory tone to the text that is disclosed within even the opening few paragraphs of the story, as reference is made to the 'peculiarities' of Ruthven's appearance, typifies the Gothic of this period. Specific and explicit reference is made to the oddness of Ruthven's 'dead grey eye' that emits a 'leaden ray'[34] over all that it looks upon, and of course it was to the monster's 'dull yellow eye'[35] that readers of *Frankenstein* were first made aware of. The eye also held similar sinister connotations in William Beckford's 1782 French novel *Vathek*, whereby the villain (Vathek himself) was in possession of an eye that when angry 'became so terrible, that no person could bear to behold it; and the wretch upon whom it was fixed, instantly fell backward, and sometimes expired.'[36] Should Polidori's readers have failed to pay sufficient attention to the less than subtle hints as to the danger that lurks within the enigmatic Lord, he ensures that the true extent of Ruthven's evil is revealed through the explicitly worded correspondence that Aubrey receives whilst residing in Rome.

There is inherent within both *The Vampyre* and *Frankenstein* (although arguably more so in *Frankenstein*) the suggestion that there is definite danger in realising the full scientific potential of the period in which they were written as the characters within each text operate without moral or legal boundary and receive no formal punishment or ramification for their deeds. Whilst it could be argued that Frankenstein's guilt and suffering towards the end of the text is punishment enough, these feelings of guilt are in no way sufficient enough to exonerate him from the very wrongs that he has *chosen* to commit. If we are looking for evidence of cultural context within each of the texts then it would seem that we would find it within the concept of free will or unchecked ambition that dominates each text. In a period of such rapid and unprecedented development as was the Industrial Revolution in Britain, both Shelley and Polidori could be regarded as appealing for the reining in of desire and seeking some degree of responsibility to be taken by those who seemingly push the boundaries of science and life without due regard or respect for the consequences and suffering that may be caused.

In the masculine and scientifically driven period in which these two texts were written it is also interesting to note the complete absence of feisty women within the texts. Arguably both Elizabeth and Miss Aubrey serve purpose only as victims whose fates are sealed, so to speak, long before either text reaches its conclusion. Unlike earlier Gothic writing in which women were often cast as conduits for ensuring ancestral lineage, a privilege or reward often granted to them once they had overcome whatever particular danger the story detailed, the women in both *The Vampyre* and *Frankenstein* are more (if indeed it is possible to be so) marginalised by late Georgian powerful patriarchal society. Effectively both Elizabeth and Miss Aubrey remain entirely innocent throughout each novel, becoming expendable and serving only as a means of permitting the villains to exact revenge. Throughout the duration of each text these women remain in ignorance of the dangers that surround them and consequently are unequipped to deal with the threat as it advances upon them.

Certainly it seems that the ability to survive in each of these novels is entirely dependent upon the way in which and the extent to which information is divulged. Whereas Aubrey at least tries to warn against the threat of Ruthven (his advice however, is largely unheeded and Ruthven remains at large to prey upon his victims), Victor Frankenstein takes an altogether different approach – that of saying nothing – and is all the more despicable for that.

The Victorian Vampire – Social Taboo and the Return of the Repressed

Just how well information can be put to good use and the way in which it can shape the outcome of a text is very much evident in Bram Stoker's 1897 novel *Dracula*. Therefore it is to *Dracula* and also another vampire tale, Sheridan Le Fanu's *Carmilla* that this chapter shall move next. By the time *Carmilla* was published in 1871 the reading public were familiar with stories featuring a great many of those 'monsters' that we accept as being Gothic fodder today. Certainly tales of vampires, ghosts, animated corpses, premature burial (a particular favourite of Poe) and isolated, tortured souls were plentiful and each one little more than a variation upon a theme, featuring extensively in publications such as the *London Magazine* and *New Monthly*. What is worth considering however, is that in creating such a physical 'other' to become the villain the Gothic managed to move away almost entirely from the concept of the fallibility of man that characterised the first phase form of the genre. It is at this point in its somewhat complicated history that the Gothic and its monsters begin to depict 'imaginings of the not-self engaged in a struggle at the border of experience'[37] rather than relying absolutely upon the feelings and capabilities (no matter how heinous) of mortal man.

As would be expected, both *Carmilla* and *Dracula* do have distinct common features that separate them from the very earliest vampire fiction as typified by Polidori. In the first instance each of these novels mark a return to traditional Gothic in terms of the locations in which they both are set; as can be seen when considering the opening few paragraphs of *Carmilla* and the anonymous castle in which the action takes place:

> It stands on a slight eminence in a forest. The road, very old and narrow,
> passes in front of its drawbridge...Over all this the schloss shows its
> many-windowed front; its towers and its Gothic chapel...and at the right
> a steep Gothic bridge carries the road over a stream that winds in deep
> shadow through the wood.[38]

Certainly Le Fanu's atmospheric spoiler leaves the reader in no doubt as to what type of tale they are about to read and a similar sense of foreboding and forewarning is employed by Stoker as Harker details his own somewhat sinister and troubling approach to Castle Dracula:

> There were dark rolling, clouds overhead, and in the air the heavy,
> oppressive sense of thunder...I felt a strange chill, and a lonely feeling

came over me...Suddenly I became conscious of the fact that the driver was in the act of pulling up the horses in the courtyard of a vast ruined castle, from whose tall black windows came no ray of light, and whose broken battlements showed a jagged line against the moonlit sky.[39]

Both texts also make a significant movement forward in the levels of sexuality and eroticism that they portray. There was, of course, a distinct sense of sexual motivation behind the behaviour of Lord Ruthven in Polidori's *The Vampyre*, but essentially Ruthven was a caddish libertine whose vampiristic tendencies appeared more as a metaphor for the sexual behaviour and attitude displayed by Ruthven rather than as evidence of him actually being a vampire per se. Schedoni and Ambrosio were similarly afflicted by carnal cravings, but the degrees of physical attractions and lusts that they experienced were similarly not akin to the *absolute* desire that is felt by both the Count and Carmilla, whose vampire cravings are absolutely linked to their lives and to their very existences and not at all representative of fad or of whimsy.

Whereas Ruthven operates as 'the conventional rakehell or libertine with a few vampiric attributes grafted on to him' whose 'vampirism is merely a continuation of rakery by other means'[40], the Count is a different breed of vampire altogether. In Polidori's early vampire novel the metaphor is quite simple to understand as is the overall message of the text, which is to high-light the inherent dangers of libertinism. This is clearly readable through the irresponsible way in which the vampire Ruthven behaves, and there is indeed scope to support the assertion that 'for Polidori, the 'vampire story' is conceived as a variant upon the moral tale, a tale designed principally as a *warning* – here, against the fascinating power of...libertinism.'[41]

Quite obviously this is not the case in either *Dracula* or *Carmilla*, as the vampires in these texts are exclusively motivated and driven by their vampire cravings and their physical *need* for blood. They cease to be metaphors in the way that Ruthven was and become instead real (within the boundaries of willing suspension of disbelief) Gothic monsters. This said however, it would be an error of judgement to assume that in light of this their blood lusts are far from purely functional; to the contrary their 'drinking' is heavily sexualised and the act of blood taking is met with enthusiasm and sublime pleasure. Consequently both texts are heavily sexually and erotically charged with this sexuality demonstrating both heterosexual and homosexual intent.

With this in mind it is certainly not beyond the realms of reason to assume that both Le Fanu and Stoker were deliberately liberating the most forbidden social and sexual impulses of the Victorian era. In an age of such strong morality and prudery that labelled behaviour such as that found in both *Carmilla* and *Dracula* as criminal, it is indeed plausible that writers found in returning to the Gothic (specifically the way in which the genre has been seen to offer distance from real time and real events) the opportunity to explore these impulses in a manner that would thus avoid censorship or social ramification. Certainly it is possible to interpret the behaviour of the vampires in each of these stories as 'liberating the most forbidden social impulses'[42] and that by means of ensuring a happy ending whereby the vampire is destroyed these Gothic novelists were seeking at once to offer 'conventional happy endings [whilst] reassuring their readers at the same time that all was right with the world.'[43]

Having identified the 'boundary pushing' aspect behind each of these novels, it is seems somewhat regressive to go on to mention the return to traditional Gothic form that both Le Fanu and Stoker offer, whereby at the end of each novel the threats are eliminated and satisfactory return to the natural order is achieved. Nevertheless this is what each of these authors do, and perhaps this is less to do with the desire of the authors to communicate cultural anxieties or to press fear upon their readers regarding social context and more to do with the concept that without such conventional endings the evident sexual 'deviancy' of the plots would have proved to be too immoral a conclusion for a prudish Victorian audience to entertain.

When we consider the endings of the texts, specifically the way in which the threat is removed and the vampire destroyed in *Dracula*, we also need to explore the role that Mina Harker holds within the text, for without her it is quite possible that the Count's escape would have been successful and he would be free to return to Transylvania and re-group before launching another attack upon British soil. In refusing to perceive herself as helpless victim Mina Harker willingly injects herself into the hunt and her ability to 'communicate' with the vampire proves to be indispensible in hunting him down. She seizes control of her destiny in much more gutsy fashion that we have seen in any female character in the Gothic thus far and her courage is ultimately rewarded as she is freed from Dracula's grasp and she is able to continue her life with Jonathan and start a family with him.

Without a doubt *Dracula* is a complex novel and open to a number of different readings and interpretations – psychological, supernatural, religious, sexual, social – and there is definitely much more at work than simple good versus evil. On the one hand the novel deals with the absolute threat to humanity that the army of blood-sucking vampires that Dracula is creating pose, and at the same time appears to suggest that Dracula himself represents the 'return of the repressed'[44] in human nature and that the lust for 'power and domination'[45] that the Count demonstrates is a clear warning of the dangers of living in a modern and secular society.

It would certainly seem that Stoker, like so many of his Gothic predecessors, has successfully managed to offer a degree of speculation as to the face of the society that he witnesses around him and incorporate this insight into a Gothic story that at first glance appears to be little more than formulaic writing. It is because of this seeming duality of purpose and intent (that is to tell a fictional story whilst at the same time detailing and recording real events) that the Gothic becomes such a complex genre to understand. Whilst it *is* possible to take many of the texts studied hereto at face value and to enjoy them for the stories they are, it also needs to be stressed that they are more than simply the sum of their very basic-looking parts. Arguably it is the *potential* of the genre to allow unspoken thoughts to be heard that has permitted its longevity and allure.

In Conclusion

Why, though, should this be the case? What is it about the psychology of the Gothic that has allowed so many writers over such a great period of time to manipulate the genre to suit their own purposes? Certainly the answer to this question will go a long way to understanding and explaining the role that the Gothic has within modern crime fiction, which is of course the central preoccupation of this book.

The answer, superficially at least, is obvious – and that is that the Gothic centres on the concept of fear, and thus any form of writing that engages, albeit even slightly, with the issue of fear, will find a willing host within the Gothic genre. Fear is a basic human instinct, often the primary and overwhelming response to anything new that is not understood. Despite labelling it basic, however, it would be wrong to assume that fear is in any way a simple phenomenon to understand. The nature of human fear – the way that we respond to it and the way in which we must engage with it in order to move forward and thus conquer our fears – has always been and will continue to be a rich source of material for the Gothic novel.

Demonstrably those periods throughout history when the Gothic has particularly flourished are periods of strong cultural change, and thus are periods when society was at its most likely to be experiencing a wide range of fears and paranoia. The concept that the rise of the Gothic can be linked to social and historical context is indeed an interesting concept and there are certainly specific periods in British history where the Gothic does appear to flourish. One such period, as has just been discussed, is the scientifically charged Victorian era that produced *Dracula* (1897) and *The Strange Case of Dr Jekyll and Mr Hyde* (1886). Arguably 'it was in the context of Victorian science, society and culture that [the] fictional power' of texts such as these 'was possible, [as they were] associated with anxieties about the stability of the social and domestic order and the effects of economic and scientific rationality.'[46]

In continuing to recount the history of the Gothic genre and understanding how revivals and flourishes within the genre relate to social context, specifically the scientific advancements of a particular era it is important to mention the origins of the apocalyptical or post-apocalyptic novel. If we are to understand the rise of these texts as a direct consequence of 'the prevalence of scientific devices and experiments as causes of tales and horror'[47], then it becomes instantly apparent why writing of this nature would find a degree of natural affinity within the Gothic. Certainly 'the loss of human identity and the alienation of self from both itself and the social bearings in which a sense of reality is secured'[48] that a great many of these novels address is closely linked to the fundamental need for procreation and maintenance of identity through familial lineage that was present in much first phase Gothic writing. If we substitute aggressive villains or Gothic monsters for the 'threatening shapes of increasingly dehumanised environments, machines doubles and violent, psychotic fragmentation'[49] that we find in the apocalyptic novel then it becomes quite clear that the Gothic and the apocalyptic novel have much in common.

Interestingly the first novel of this kind appeared as far back as 1826, and was written by Mary Shelley. In *The Last Man* Shelley reverts to traditional Gothic form whereby she purports that the text is her edited account of documents from a future world that has been overrun by a plague and humankind all but destroyed. Despite the fact that the novel was ill received at the time, it did nevertheless begin a trend for a number of novels each depicting the end of mankind and of the world for a variety of different reasons. One significant follow-up to the Shelley text was Richard Jefferies' 1885 novel *After London*, which details the attempts made by the few human beings that manage to survive the catastrophe that has already occurred at the start of the text.

A somewhat better known example of this form of writing is H. G. Wells' *The War of the Worlds*, a text that is radically different from its predecessors in that the threat to mankind results from alien invasion rather than natural catastrophe. Some three years later in 1901 Matthew Phipps Shiel's novel *The Purple Cloud* appeared and since then novels of this type have been produced in vast numbers. Successful box office hits such as *28 Days Later*, *The Village of the Damned*, *Dawn of the Dead* (remake) all demonstrate just how strong the public desire for fiction of this type remains.

One of the better examples of apocalyptic writing and Gothic-driven science fiction to demonstrate the way in which the Gothic influence manifests itself is Richard Matheson's 1954 novel *I Am Legend*. Set in the future (Matheson's future – the novel takes place in 1976) the main plot revolves around Robert Neville, possibly the only human still alive in a world now populated by vampires.

As the novel opens Neville is found to be repairing and barricading his house in preparation for the vampire attack that will occur as soon as night falls. In his fortress-like abode Neville contemplates the struggle to find a place for himself in the world, or indeed the purpose of a future in which humanity as he understands it is lost.

The horror of the text lies less in the presence of the vampires themselves, and more in Neville's utter isolation as he attempts to doggedly go about his daily rituals of securing the house, checking generators, looking for food and slaying vampires. The desperation of his plight is not lost on him either:

Why *not* go out? It was a sure way to be free of them.

Be one of them.

He chuckled at the simplicity of it, then shoved himself up and walked crookedly to the bar. Why not? His mind plodded on. Why go through all this complexity when a flung-open door and a few steps would end it all?[50]

There is a distinct Gothic element to Neville's desire to *survive* and to protect his human identity even if it turns out that he is indeed the only human left in the world, and his dogged determination to survive links to the earliest of Gothic texts as it is pitched against the dogged *desire* of the vampires to destroy him. It reminds us of Isabella's desperate flight from Manfred just as much as it does Van Helsing and his accomplices' determination to slay Count Dracula. The fight against the monster (whatever form the monster takes) has always been a core part of the Gothic and Matheson's text is no exception.

Where this novel differs from any of the texts studied hereto, however, is the absolute loss of humanity at the end of the text following Neville's death. That Neville should be regarded as such a deviant and so feared because he is human and not one of the infected is a theme that thus far the Gothic had not engaged with. In this text it is Neville, rather than the monsters who becomes the 'other' and whilst the concept of 'otherness' is basic fodder for the Gothic there is within this particular text complete reversal of all that we have come to expect from the genre so far. For the most part it is always the human race, those who demonstrate goodness and morality who are the victors, but in this new form of writing it appears that we cannot take even this for granted anymore.

Without doubt identifying and understanding cultural context is an integral part of understanding the Gothic itself, but it is important, however, not to take this theory to the extreme, and to assume that the Gothic only appears at times of crisis. This is not the case, and there is an equally strong argument for the Gothic having nothing at all to do with its cultural context. That there are these two opposing theories regarding the understanding the ongoing rise and fall of the Gothic is something that can be expressed quite succinctly; that on the one hand, there is always a valid historical interpretation of a particular text, but on the other too is equally appealing belief in 'the idea of gothic as a 'tendency' in human thought, feelings, and modes of expression, rather than one limited to particular places or times.'[51]

Over time the Gothic has become a genre that is adaptable and amenable, able to be used with effect within a range of different genres, and certainly this flexibility is vital in accounting for the genre remaining such a distinct and recognisable form of writing. In understanding the rise of the Gothic, its tropes and motifs, its influence and capabilities, it should come as no surprise that modern crime fiction should have its roots so firmly based in the genre. Demonstrably when handled correctly the Gothic and crime fiction combine to make perfect bed-mates and it is difficult to imagine modern crime fiction existing as it does today without the heavy influence of Gothic fiction.

CHAPTER TWO

Early American Gothic and the Birth of a Genre? Detective Trace in Poe's Gothic Writing

T O suggest that the development of the Gothic genre was in any way linear or sequential or indeed that it followed any sort of set path is to be far too simplistic and it is more appropriate to regard the growth of the genre as developing 'slowly and discontinuously'[52]. Whilst it is possible to piece together some form of a family tree for the genre with a degree of accuracy, the matter is further confused when the advent of the American form is brought into the equation as it was not only on *this* side of the Atlantic that Gothic writing flourished: by the mid-19th century the Gothic form in America had truly taken shape. Essentially it was Brockden Brown, Hawthorne and Poe who were for the most part responsible for reforming the genre for the American audience. Whilst Brockden Brown and Hawthorne created a tone for the genre that was more American in outlook, Poe managed to offer yet another direction for the genre that managed to combine features of both British and the newly emerging American Gothic.

Of these three it is Poe who wrote the most prolifically and it is his manipulation of the genre that makes him the key focus of this chapter. Essentially Poe altered the dynamics of the British Gothic form in two distinct ways. The first was the greater emphasis that he placed upon giving voice to the psychological forces at work within his characters (an insight generated by Poe's frequent use of first person narration) and the second the move into the realms of detective fiction that can be seen in several of his short stories; this gives the same insight into motivations and psychology but through third-person narrative.

Before looking to Poe directly it is important to take the time to understand the way in which the Gothic form developed in America and in just what ways it proved different to earlier, British writing. Two examples of early American Gothic writing by Nathaniel Hawthorne (*The House of the Seven Gables* and *The White Old Maid*) offer some insight into how exactly the genre was reshaped by this particular American writer.

Early American Gothic: Hawthorne's *The House of the Seven Gables* and *The White Old Maid*

American Gothic differs from the British type for the most part in its shift away from heightened sensationalism and melodrama into texts that are much more sombre in tone, concerned not so much with the sense of mania that pervaded so much of the earlier British writing, but more so with psychological and social dysfunction. This shift in pace and mood is very much evident in Hawthorne's *House of the Seven Gables* (1851).

For a number of different reasons this text in particular demonstrates the most significant differences between British and American Gothic. If we look to the very way in which the novel opens we can see that the American writing has a very different style to its British equivalent:

> Halfway down a bystreet of one of our New England towns stands a rusty wooden house, with seven acutely peaked gables, facing towards various points of the compass, and a huge, clustered chimney in the midst. The street is Pyncheon Street; the house is the old Pyncheon House...[53]

When compared to the opening of Scottish writer Allan Cunningham's 1831 *The Master of Logan*, the difference in tone, atmosphere and unease becomes apparent:

> One summer's eve, as I passed through a burial-ground on the banks of the Nith, I saw an old man resting on a broad flat stone which covered a grave. The church itself was gone and but a matter of memory: yet the church-yard was still reverentially preserved, and families of name and standing continued to inter in the same place with their fathers. Some one had that day been buried, and less care than is usual had been taken in closing up the grave, for, as I went forward, my foot struck the fragment of a bone.[54]

Aside from the fact that within the Hawthorne text there is no castle to speak of (ancestral castles being an almost unheard of feature in the New World) or indeed no traditional Gothic setting such as an abandoned church or graveyard, what is notably different from this description of the house than any other location that we have come across in British texts is the complete absence of anything outwardly terrifying or threatening as regards the location that is being described. Instead Hawthorne appears to be rejecting this particular aspect of traditional Gothic and the alternative is significantly more subtle in its approach:

> Thus the great house was built. Familiar as it stands in the writer's recollection – for it has been an object of curiosity with him from boyhood, both as a specimen of the best and stateliest architecture of a long-past epoch, and as the scene of events more full of human interest, perhaps, than those of a gray feudal castle – familiar as it stands, in its rusty old age.[55]

The reality of the matter is however rarely as simple as it first seems, this is after all still a Gothic text, and in due course the Pyncheon house is revealed to harbour secrets that are just as threatening and sinister as the castles and ancestral homes of early British Gothic. The key difference between this American text and its British counterparts however, is that the castles and homes of British texts have no degree of personification or threat attached to them *themselves*, and instead it is all to do with the villains that inhabit them. In *The House of the Seven Gables* it is very much the *house* that carries the threat and the memory of all that has passed between its walls. Put simply, without Manfred, Otranto is nothing; merely an average castle. Yes, it has vaults and underground passages, but without the villain these cease to hold any form of danger. The Pyncheon house on the other hand is very much the sum of its parts; mysterious and affecting, capable of 'expressing…vicissitudes that have passed within.'[56]

In replacing the sinister setting that was such a trademark of earlier British Gothic writing, there is a degree of danger that the tone of the genre as a whole will be altered and much of the suspense lost. British texts were often dramatised and made successful by the mania and frenzy that the very physical space of the castle provided, and what we are presented with in this particular example of early American Gothic is a location that is character-ized by an over-riding sense of gloom and a feeling of tiredness in which there is no suspense generated and the text becomes much more sedate in tone. This complete absence of suspense within the text has led to harsh criticism of the story that suggest 'there is almost no story to *The House of the Seven Gables*', and that in the absence of story and pace effectively there is no 'suspense' to the narrative and that as a result of this the story fails[57].

It is a harsh assessment, but one that is not altogether unfair. For the most part the narrative does indeed plod along at a gentle pace and much traditional British Gothic convention is replaced with a number of alternative stylistic approaches that are more pertinent to the American audience:

> Though the grand gloom of European Gothic was inappropriate, the commonplace of American culture was full of little mysteries and guilty secrets from communal and family pasts...The newness of the American world, however, retained some shadows of superstitious fancy which appeared in concerns with the relation of the individual, mentally and politically, to social and religious forms of order. The negotiation with fictions of the past, as both a perpetuation and disavowal of superstitious fears and habits, attempts to banish certain shadows haunting the American daylight and discovers new dark shapes.[58]

That the house is shown to be haunted and that is becomes such a physical link to the people that live within it ensures that *The House of the Seven Gables* belongs to the emerging theme of the 'old dark house' within American Gothic, whereby houses become physically affected by the evil or wrongdoing that occurs within them. Of course one of the earliest and best examples of an 'old dark house' text is Poe's *The Fall of the House of Usher* which will be discussed later in this chapter. What Poe does so superbly in *Usher* however, is to expose the complex relationship that exists between the *self* and the *house* within the Gothic and demonstrate how each of these states can be made to 'merge...into a single image of terror.'[59] Another text that makes similarly effective use of the 'old dark house' is Le Fanu's *The Wyvern Mystery* (1869). Mary Roberts Rinehart's considerably later *The Circular Staircase* (1908) is a further example that showcases the features of the genre wonderfully.

This said however, there are aspects to Hawthorne's text that *do* bear distinct resemblance to British Gothic writing as we have come to recognise it. Certainly the theme of ownership and true blood lineage with regards the family home is a feature of the earliest Gothic writing of Walpole and Reeve, and in Hawthorne's text we learn that the Pyncheon House has been built upon land that came into Pyncheon hands under questionable behaviour. The death of the true owner of the land, the bizarre prophecy that he utters as he dies and the subsequent passing of the land into hands in which it did not rightly belong are core elements of traditional Gothic and each of them are to be found in Hawthorne's text.

Like many earlier Gothic texts the novel is as much to do with issues of class as it is to do with the restoration of order. To this effect both Hepzibah and Clifford become innocent victims of sins committed before their time, namely the acquisition of the Maule land by the unscrupulous Colonel Pyncheon. Having fallen upon hard financial times they are forced to live solitary existences, shunned and mocked by neighbours and townsfolk, unable to escape the confines of the house, and consequently they provide living examples of how the sins of the fathers (and forefathers) shall fall upon the children.

In terms of its most predominant theme the novel has a great deal to do with the colonisation of America, specifically the way in which land was perceived to have been stolen, or acquired erroneously in the past. In light of this it is possible to interpret Hepzibah's reclusive and socially insecure behaviour as a manifestation of the guilt that she feels at her ancestors' behaviour. The position that she holds within the text is one of a victim forced to live under the heavy weight and burden of previous wrong-doing whilst all the time having to act as the hero who will avert financial ruin and save the Pyncheon fate. This simultaneous victim-hero role of Hepzibah's character is probably the most interesting aspect of the whole novel, personifying as it does the book's uneasy tone. This unease is of course resolved at the end of the text in true Gothic tradition whereby the Houses of Pyncheon and Maule are brought together happily and more importantly, *under free will*, by the marriage between Phoebe Pyncheon and Holgrave, mysterious descendant and heir of Matthew Maule.

Hawthorne's writing is deeply laced with concerns over morality, characters and actions that are either morally right or wrong. Much of the novel's narrative surrounds Hepzibah's daily struggle to overcome the isolation, guilt and anxiety that she experiences as a result of continuing to live in the house that represents the great sin that has been committed by Colonel Pyncheon. In traditional Gothic style Hepzibah's home, that which should provide comfort and safety is revealed to hold neither of these things; the house, rather like Hepzibah herself, faces impending ruin.

However, despite having such strong Gothic roots, the potential of *The House of the Seven Gables* seems never to be fully reached, and in this respect the criticism that there is no story to the narrative remains a fair assessment. In a novel in which the great sin and the wrongness has already occurred before the actual story begins, there is only so much pace and suspense that can be generated and maintained unless a significant event occurs (which it does not) that requires the interjection of a little more frenzy. It would seem that in concentrating his narrative on the fallout of events past rather than including the occurrence of the events themselves, Hawthorne has perhaps unintentionally fallen into one of the pitfalls of removing the key event that not only sets up, but also shapes the direction of the text, and that is the very real danger of losing the *story* of the novel and detailing instead a narrative in which almost nothing interesting happens.

There is a similar notable absence of both story and action in one of Hawthorne's lesser studied short stories, *The White Old Maid* (1835). This short story precedes *The House of the Seven Gables* by some 16 years and because of this can be regarded as an early attempt by Hawthorne to inject British Gothic into an American arena. Opening with suitable Gothic charm the tale is set in a lavishly furnished chamber within an old mansion. The difference in the tone of the opening of this example and the presence of distinct Gothic trace when compared to that of *The House of the Seven Gables* is indeed marked, and we can compare the two:

> The moonbeams came through two deep and narrow windows, and
> showed a spacious chamber richly furnished in an antique fashion. From
> one lattice the shadow of the diamond panes was thrown upon the floor:
> the ghostly light, through the other, slept upon a bed, falling between
> the heavy silken curtains, and illuminating the face of a young man. But,
> how quietly the slumberer lay! How pale his features! And how like a
> shroud the sheet was wound about his frame! Yes; it was a corpse, in its
> burial clothes.[60]

Subsequently two young women enter the chamber and the suggestion is made that whilst the young man was still alive the two women were involved in a battle for his attentions and affections. Unable to resolve the conflict they agree to meet in the chamber once again at some allotted time in the future and forgiveness and resolution will only be reached depending upon the level of suffering that each woman has endured in the years between this night and that which they decide upon in the future. The fact that both women are to endure such a degree of suffering does of course link this particular example back to earlier British texts that were given Gothic credibility by the presence of both desire and suffering, but it would seem that in the American form of the genre there is a marked reduction in the degree of *desire* that is present in any of the texts, rather characters are given substance and sustainability based purely upon the *suffering* that they endure that occurred through no fault of their own.

Already Hawthorne has set up two interesting aspects to his story; the original event that has caused the disagreement and also the future event that will determine the extent to which this disagreement can be resolved. But bizarrely at no point within the text are either of these two crucial aspects ever developed; not only do we never find out what has passed between the two women and the young man, equally we never find out what passes between them when they meet again. In attempting to generate an air of mystery within his writing it seems that Hawthorne has perhaps taken things a step too far; and by removing information regarding the key events has managed only to produce a short story that details very little more than the peculiar funerary obsession of an odd old woman swathed in white.

Poe's Gothic: British and American Motif Combined

If we take the central theme of Hawthorne's tale to be betrayal of some form, then it is interesting to compare it with Poe's equally short story *The Cask of Amontillado* (1846). Although there is no love triangle within Poe's text to speak of, it does, nevertheless, revolve around betrayal, specifically Fortunato's betrayal of the narrator. Like *The White Old Maid* the details of the betrayal are never actually revealed to the reader, but it is interesting that in Poe's tale, unlike in Hawthorne's, this doesn't actually seem to matter. At no point in the very brief tale does our enjoyment of it become any less because we remain in the dark and the specifics of the original event are kept from us.

Why should this be the case? What is so very different about Poe's handling of the narrative that makes his short story a success when Hawthorne's similar tale falls short? In the first instance there is huge difference between the pace of the two texts. Whereas Hawthorne gradually introduces us to his characters, Poe sets his stall up so to speak within the very first sentence: 'The thousand injuries of Fortunato I had borne as best I could; but when he ventured upon insult, I vowed revenge.'[61]

That Poe has chosen to use first person narration also offers a distinct advantage in the instant access to the narrator's thoughts and feelings that such narrative technique allows. The narrator in *The Cask of Amontillado* becomes instantly more appealing as we are permitted to hear first hand not only the actual conversations that take place between himself and the somewhat unfortunate Fortunato, but also because we gain such a degree of insight into his psychology and motivations. In contrast, because we know nothing about any of the characters in *The White Old Maid* we care very little for them and consequently much interest in the story is lost. Unfortunately Hawthorne has not replaced this lack of detail in his characters with detail in any other aspect of his text, and the result of this is an absolute nothingness of story whose characters and eventual outcome we have little interest in.

What Poe has done instead it seems is to give his readers just enough information in the first few sentences to whet their appetites and then rapidly advance the tale to the point at which the revenge is carried out and the treacherous Fortunato is buried alive within the walls of the cellar. Whereas Poe's tale is full of action and detail, Hawthorne's is markedly lacking in either and this lack of detail is absolutely detrimental to the success of *his* story.

That there is such a great difference between the writing styles of Poe and Hawthorne does make it difficult to compare them in terms of their status as key players in the development of American Gothic. Whereas Hawthorne's writing is much more sedate in tone, Poe is demonstrably a greater fan of flights of fancy and uncapped madness that make his short stories much more entertaining to read. Having said this, however, it would be wrong to assume that simply because Poe demonstrates seeming wild abandon in his writings that there is no *craft* behind them. On the contrary it would seem that Poe manages to combine this aspect of traditional British Gothic with the more American tendency to include psychological depth of character to great effect.

The successful way in which this marriage of British and American motif works can be seen in one of his earlier short stories, *The Tell-Tale Heart*. Like *The Cask of Amontillado* and a great many of Poe's short stories it also is written in the first person and catapults us straight into the action from the very first sentence:

> TRUE! – nervous – very, very dreadfully nervous I had been and am; but why *will* you say that I am mad? The disease had sharpened my senses – not destroyed – not dulled them. Above all was the sense of hearing acute. I heard all things in the heaven and in the earth. I heard many things in hell.[62]

Throughout the short narrative this heady pace is maintained and at no point does Poe digress from the task in hand that is to tell the story of the murder and the overwhelming and terrifying manner in which the narrator is overcome by his guilt, demonstrating all the signs of mania and madness that defined the villains of traditional British Gothic. Like Manfred, Ambrosio, Schedoni and Victor Frankenstein the narrator *here* is also driven by impulse, obsession and sheer *desire* in which there is no time or room for manoeuvre, second thought or regret.

Like those villains who went before him the narrator in *The Tell-Tale Heart* becomes consumed by the 'mission' that he has set for himself. Unable to think about anything else and, having seized upon the idea, he must pursue it until the bitter end. Combine this with the greater proximity to the narrator's thoughts and feelings that is generated by the use of the first person and we can begin to understand why the tale is so chilling.

The tale becomes all the more unsettling given the motivation for the murder that the narrator reveals to us:

> I think it was his eye! yes, it was this! One of his eyes resembled that
> of a vulture – a pale blue eye, with a film over it. Whenever it fell upon
> me, my blood ran cold; and so by degrees – very gradually – I made up
> my mind to take the life of the old man, and thus rid myself of the eye
> forever.[63]

Aside from the obvious links to early British Gothic in the reference to and significance attached to the 'eye', the tale becomes all the more unsettling because despite the obvious unattractiveness of the eye, when it comes to motivation for murder it simply is no *genuine* motivation at all; after all, who murders and dismembers someone simply because they happen to have an ugly blue eye? Almost all of the villains identified and studied hereto, despite how abhorrent their crimes and misdemeanors may have been, at least had some degree of logical motivation to account for their behaviour, be it the desire for an heir or the want of land or wealth. There was a clear sense of *what* and *why* present to account for their actions, but this sense of logic is entirely absent from Poe's text, and despite the narrator's many protestations of being completely sane we can safely assume that he and sanity are many miles apart.

Consequently and with hindsight the extent to which the villains of early Gothic were singularly dimensional characters can quite clearly be seen. Relatively easy to understand, the likes of Manfred and Walter Lovel demonstrate no complexity of personality, no sub-conscious or multi-layered aspect to their characters – they simply are what they are and their behaviour can be understood in that they see, they want and they take by whatever means necessary. The narrator in Poe's tale is different altogether; consider the hypocrisy and deliberately misleading behaviour he displays: 'I was never kinder to the old man that during the whole week before I killed him.'[64] This level of premeditation demonstrates a new facet to the structure of the Gothic villain that was only beginning to be touched upon by writers such as Shelley and Stoker and certainly demonstrates the ways in which Poe's contributions to American Gothic begin to call for a much greater significance to be placed upon the psychological representation of the forces at work within its characters.

That the narrator in *The Tell-Tale Heart* demonstrates the capacity for falsehood and deception to such an extent is indeed a new direction for the Gothic, but it is not a defining feature of Poe's work. To the contrary he explores every aspect of psychological reasoning (justified or not) in his writing. If we consider the contrast in revelation of motivation between the narrator of *The Tell-Heart Heart* and *The Black Cat* we can see just two of the many different explorations into human psychology that Poe explores in his writing:

> I slipped a noose about its neck and hung it to the limb of a tree; – hung it with the tears streaming from my eyes, and with the bitterest remorse at my heart; – hung it *because* I knew that it had loved me, and *because* I felt it had given me no reason of offence; – hung it *because* I knew that in doing so I was committing a sin...[65]

In an attempt to rationalise his behaviour the narrator ask us 'Who has not, a hundred times, found himself committing a vile or silly action, for no other reason than because he knows he should *not*?'[66]

It is this level of explanation of motivation and intent that demonstrates the ways in which Poe was able to move the complexity and make-up of the Gothic villain forward. By repackaging and portraying the villain less as a *villain* and more as a *criminal* (coupling this with details of criminal intent and of confession), the ways in which Poe contributes so significantly to the development of detective fiction (and subsequently, modern crime fiction) are easily seen. Certainly the increased focus upon *crime* within Poe's writing provide the strongest evidence for the development of detective fiction if we are to accept that detective fiction ultimately grew out of the Gothic form. In Poe's writing focus and attention cease to be a third-person account of horrors that have occurred at some prior point in history, and instead are focused very much on the *here* and *now* of the moment. This gives his tales a source of drama and mania that differs from traditional Gothic writing, but is by no means any less effective.

Poe's work, particularly his Gothic work has often been criticised for having a great propensity for 'endlessly rehearsed'[67] themes, and one of the themes that this is true of is that of horror and death or, specifically, death by horrific means. Whilst it would be misleading to suggest that earlier Gothic writing did not feature horrific crime and murder, it would be true to state that the actual details of the crimes are seldom lingered over and rarely is attention drawn to them above and beyond the detailing that is imperative to the fluidity of the plot. Poe's work on the other hand, *does* demonstrate increased focus upon death, particularly the *manner* of dying that befalls his characters and this is something that simply was not present in earlier, British Gothic writing. Whereas 'early English writers of Gothic fiction may have dealt in terrible goings-on…they did not linger over death and showed little interest in its rituals'[68], there is often more than a touch of voyeurism and sublime pleasure in the relish with which Poe details the intimacies of the crimes that he is revealing.

Certainly there is more than a simple air of relish and deliberation evident in the narrator's entombment of Fortunato in *The Cask of Amontillado*. The punishment that the narrator feels Fortunato deserves for his treachery is one that has evidently been planned carefully and deemed appropriate for the wrongs done. In considering the level of enjoyment, satisfaction and relish that the perpetrators in a great number of Poe's tales display in recounting their actions, it can be seen that this behaviour often amounts to little more than showmanship, as is evident in the narrator's recount of the murder of the old man in *The Tell-Tale Heart*:

> He shrieked once – once only. In an instant I dragged him to the floor, and pulled the heavy bed over him. I then smiled gaily to find the deed so far done.[69]

And the moment at which the narrator's wife meets her death in *The Black Cat* is treated with a similar degree of flippancy: 'I withdrew my arm from her grasp and buried the axe in her brain.'[70]

Another significant change that Poe brought to the Gothic form was of course the introduction of first-person narrative within the texts, and it is this that is largely responsible for the voyeuristic quality that was briefly mentioned earlier; having Gothic villains take such acute pleasure in their crimes was simply not a part of early Gothic whereby crime was to all extents and purposes, functional. On the one hand there is indeed a confessional aspect to this narrative technique, but as neither the narrator in *The Black Cat* nor *The Cask of Amontillado* display any form of remorse (quite the opposite in fact in *The Black Cat*: 'My happiness was supreme! The guilt of my dark deed disturbed me but little'[71]) it seems unlikely that Poe has used first person narrative to promote confession. What the technique does instead is to put us as reader into some sort of collaboration with the narrator, piquing our interest and exploiting our voyeuristic side. Let it be said however that there *are* moral ramifications to this, in that we have enjoyed the tale and therefore to what extent do we become less of a neutral reader and more of a confidante? And does this in turn put us in league with the narrator, burdening us with some measure of guilt?

Much has also been made of the way in which the boundaries of life and death overlap and become confused in much of Poe's work, and there is certainly evidence to suggest that Poe was very much 'obsessed by the catatonic condition in which life imitated death.'[72] Evidently Poe was well equipped to handle 'some of the leading ideas of his generation'[73] However, rather than crediting Poe with developing yet another new side to the Gothic genre here, we know from our understanding of early Gothic that inclusion of context (scientific or political or other) through explicit reference or through metaphor, is in fact no new direction for the genre, rather a continuation of something that the Gothic has always done, and that is to exploit the unknown and present it in a manner that generates fear.

The Move into Detective Fiction: A Study of C. Auguste Dupin

Perhaps the most significant change that Poe made was the development and introduction of the character of the detective to the genre; it is certainly the one that that is most crucial in understanding the historical link between the Gothic, detective fiction and the rise of modern crime fiction. The detective Dupin appears in just three of Poe's tales, but the significantly new dimension that his presence brought to the structure of the Gothic was considerable. It was the first time within Gothic writing that a crime of any sort had been subject to investigation by any form of third party and across these three stories Poe was able to sketch out the formula for detective fiction that is still recognised today.

Of course it is not enough to say that detective fiction simply grew out of the Gothic without attempting to explain why this should be so. Why did the beginnings of the genre emerge in the 1840s as opposed to say a decade earlier or later? Certainly it seems that in much the same way as the Gothic responded to cultural anxiety, detective fiction is also born of the same concerns. The mid-19th century was a period during which the general public was showing a great interest in all aspects of policing, crime and punishment and there is indeed a strong argument to suggest that detective fiction is merely the inevitable result of this fascination as Poe, and others after him, jumped upon the popular culture bandwagon of the period to produce a series of texts that would sate the public interest in all things criminal.

To put this unfathomable public interest in crime and criminals into context, let us turn our attentions for a moment to Charles Dickens' observations at the public hangings of Frederick and Maria Manning at Horsemonger Lane Gaol in November 1849. Such was the sheer volume of the spectators who had come to see the event that more than 400 policemen were required to control the bloodthirsty witnesses, and after the event Dickens was compelled to write the following:

> I believe that a sight so inconceivably awful as the wickedness and levity
> of the immense crowd collected at the execution could be imagined
> by no man, and could be presented n no heathen land under the sun.
> The horrors of the gibbet and of the crime which brought the wretched
> murderers to it faded in my mind before the atrocious bearing, looks and
> language of the assembled spectators.[74]

The execution of the Mannings and the crowd that it attracted was by no means a one-off event; similar volumes of spectators are recorded with great frequency at public hangings at both Horsemonger Lane Gaol and at Newgate Prison. The 1824 hanging of London banker Henry Fauntleroy at Newgate is reported to have attracted a crowd of some 100,000 spectators and the double hanging of child murders John Bishop and Peter Williams in 1831 more than 40,000.

The formation of the Metropolitan Police for London in 1829 also fuelled the public's attitudes towards crime. Previously to this policing was largely a case of apprehension of the criminal(s) after the actual crime had taken place, and the great majority of these apprehensions were undertaken by the Bow Street Runners who ran the system under the direction of Bow Street Magistrates Court. Interestingly the Runners continued to provide their service to the Court for a decade after the formation of the Met Police and certainly contributed significantly to the development of the formality of the safeguarding of London's streets.

With daily newspapers such as *The Times* filled with information about victims and criminals as well as the infamous *Newgate Calendar* which recorded the details of every execution taking place at the prison, it can be well understood how the public's imagination was fuelled by the concept of 'true crime'. Perhaps unsurprisingly it was not long before the writers of the day seized upon this level of interest and it was around the 1820s that the first of what would subsequently be dubbed the 'Newgate novels' appeared. These novels are largely semi-fictional in that they took a great proportion of their plots and inspiration from the real life goings-on of the prison and the inmates that dwelt within its walls. Typically these novels are melodramatic and sensational in tone, and often perceived as low-brow and immoral due to the crimes and the levels of sexuality that are portrayed within them. Amongst the most famous authors of the Newgate novel are Edward Butler-Lytton (*Paul Clifford* (1830) and *Eugene Aram* (1832)) and William Harrison Ainsworth (*Rookwood* (1834) and *Jack Sheppard* (1839)). Interestingly Charles Dickens, who frequently attended hangings at both Newgate and Horsemonger and wrote often about his disgust at the baying and voyeuristic nature of many of the spectators that such events attracted, is himself widely perceived to be an author of just this type of novel with many perceiving his 1837 novel *Oliver Twist* to be an example of a typical Newgate novel.

Another famous fictional story to appear from this period, and one that takes inspiration from the interest in the reported crimes of the time, is that of Sweeney Todd, the barber-come-serial-killer who appeared in the 18-part penny dreadful 'romance' *The String of Pearls* published in *The People's Periodical and Family Library* between 1846–7. The story details the murders of Todd's clients (either by means of a fall through a trapdoor or having their throats slit by his razor) and the enterprise between Todd and his accomplice, neighbouring pie-shop owner Mrs. Lovett. Now the stuff of urban legend, few fictional tales have ever caught the public imagination like Sweeney Todd and it is certainly fair to say that the story was very much a product of the era in which it was conceived – that of immense public fascination with gruesome murder.

However, whilst stories (real or fictional) about crime were aplenty during this period, few were so focused upon the *detection*, or the concept of the detective in relation to these crimes, and it was not until Poe created Dupin as one who would investigate the crime for the purpose of identifying the offender that detective fiction as we understand it today began to emerge.

The first of Poe's stories to feature C. Auguste Dupin is *The Murders in the Rue Morgue* (1841), and it is the most heavily Gothicised of the three tales. Dark in tone it recounts the seemingly unsolvable crimes that are the murders of Madame L'Espanaye and her daughter Mademoiselle Camille

L'Espanaye. Like many of Poe's short stories it is written in the first person, but the narrator is not Dupin himself, merely an acquaintance, and the resulting 'sidekick' formula has been used time and time again since in much detective fiction (Holmes and Watson, Hercule Poirot and Captain Hastings, Kay Scarpetta and Pete Marino and the much more recent Lisbeth Salander and Mikael Blomkvist of Stieg Larsson's *Millennium Trilogy* to name a few).

In Dupin we are introduced to a character who, like so many of Poe's Gothic characters, lives in almost seclusion, separated somehow from the rest of society. Dwelling in a suitably Gothic 'time-eaten and grotesque mansion' the narrator defines this almost solitary existence as 'perfect', detailing that they 'existed within [them]selves alone.'[75] Dupin also has a bizarre tendency to shun daylight hours, preferring to exist and venture out only at nightfall. Interestingly these things combined at first impression seem to deprive Dupin of so many of features and virtues of the traditional hero and instead give him an almost anti-hero status from the outset. As the tale develops we learn more of Dupin's oddities; he has peculiar analytical ability, possesses intimate knowledge of others based solely upon scant acquaintance and is noted for his bizarre behaviour and pitch of speech during moments of great intuition.

The Gothic aspect to the text gains momentum when the attention moves to the actual murder of Mme L'Espanaye and her daughter. The scene for the murders is the ominously named Rue Morgue, and close inspection of the premises reveals a number of features that would quickly become common motifs of detective fiction in the future. The first of these is the seemingly sealed room, the second is the advent of a character (the sailor) who for a time is wrongly suspected of having committed the crime and lastly the dénouement where by the *actual* details of the crime are disclosed and conclusion revealed to have been reached by acute observational skill, inference and deduction. *The Murders in the Rue Morgue* also details violent and brutal murder that was increasingly becoming a staple feature of the French Revolution and post- French Revolution era Gothic (it was certainly present in *The Monk*, *Frankenstein* and *Dracula*). The mystery that surrounds not only the identification of the murderer, but also the perplexing features regarding the murders themselves is also reminiscent of the theme of mystery present in much first phase Gothic writing.

In terms of characters, the earliest forms of the (detective) genre were 'filled with archetypes and plots from preceding fiction, particularly the gothic novel.'[76] But the influence of the Gothic extends further than this, and 'is said to account for the dark settings, unfathomable motivations, and preoccupation with brilliant of unexpected solutions'[77] that typify the earliest examples of detective fiction. *Rue Morgue*, like its predecessors, also celebrates a return to order at the end of the text as the perpetrator (the orangutan in this case) is captured and detained at a nearby livery stable.

Whereas *The Murders in the Rue Morgue* echoes the violence of the Gothic, *The Purloined Letter* adopts an altogether more subtle approach and focuses instead on a psychological understanding of the central characters. Drawing upon the very recent tendency of the Gothic (American Gothic more so) to explore the inner workings of the mind and give credence to understanding psychological complexities and motivations, *The Purloined Letter* advocates the need to understand psychological motivation as a means of gaining the information necessary to solve the crime.

In pre-empting behaviour and actions Dupin is able to locate the missing document (a letter in this instance) where the Prefect had failed to do so, explaining that in order to conceal the letter in a fashion where it could be to hand and readily available at any time, the only solution was in 'not attempting to conceal it at all.'[78] Thus Dupin finds the missing letter 'hidden' within plain sight in a letter rack. Of course the locating of a document that contains some form of secret has always been a feature of the Gothic, but Poe's ability to take this aspect and to work it so effectively into the detective fiction form, demonstrates a new direction for the Gothic genre that is crucial part of understanding the development and rise of modern crime fiction.

Is it enough however, simply to accept that detective fiction owes its existence entirely to the Gothic genre and that it did not in fact emerge independently of it? In order to understand the way in which this works fully we need to ask ourselves if any of Poe's detective stories (by which I mean the three Dupin tales) would work were it not for the Gothic influence that they each display. In other words, what would happen to these tales (in terms of structure, plot and overall effect) were this Gothic influence removed?

The Gothic traits of two of Poe's detective stories have already been identified and explained; the dark mood and violence of *The Murders in the Rue Morgue* and the role of psychological understanding in *The Purloined Letter*, but if we are to attempt to interpret the motivation and intent behind Poe's writing then it would seem appropriate to take a moment to explore his own perceptions regarding the manner in which a story should be constructed. Indeed the very process behind story writing and crafting is something that Poe details in his 1846 essay *The Philosophy of Composition* and there are two points that Poe makes within this essay that are pertinent to our understanding of his detective fiction as being a logical and deliberate extension of the Gothic. The first of these is the paramount importance that he places upon determining the *effect* that he wishes the writing to have upon the reader even before he puts pen to paper. He explains that he prefers:

> ...commencing with the consideration of an *effect*...I consider whether it
> can best be wrought by incident or tone – whether by ordinary incidents
> and peculiar tone, or the converse, by peculiarity of both incident
> and tone – afterward looking about me (or rather within) for such
> combinations of event, or tone, as shall best aid me in the construction of
> the effect. [79]

With this in mind we can therefore assume that the Gothic *effects* of mystery, unease and distress have been deliberately crafted by Poe. If we also consider Poe's declaration that with regards his writing, no 'one point in its composition is referable either to accident or intuition – that the work proceeded step by step, to its completion with the precision and rigid consequence of a mathematical problem'[80], we can be fairly sure that every word, theme and idea that his stories contain have been carefully considered and put there with acute deliberation. It is an important aspect to consider, because with regard to the two stories analysed thus far it can be quite clearly seen that should the Gothic elements be removed then that which Poe defines as being of such supreme importance (effect) would be severely compromised and thus the story would fail.

Let us look at Poe's second of the three Dupin stories, *The Mystery of Marie Rogêt*. Published in 1842, the story purports to have taken place some two years after the case of the murders of the L'Espanayes had been resolved. It revolves around the disappearance and subsequent discovery of the murdered body of Marie Rogêt and although essentially a detective story it, like both *The Murders in the Rue Morgue* and *The Purloined Letter*, demonstrates Gothic motifs.

As in *The Murders in the Rue Morgue*, *Marie Rogêt* depicts violence and brutality that complete with sombre tone echo Gothic convention. As the tale progresses the extent of the brutality is revealed to us and we are drip-fed fragments of information from a number of different sources each recounting events relating to the murder. The investigation and mystery that surrounds not only the disappearance but also the death of the young victim is traditionally Gothic in concept and the manner in which these details are revealed to the reader also mimic early Gothic style in that they are revealed to us effectively third hand, gathered from newspaper articles and clippings. Being familiar with the format of many Gothic texts we are aware of the differing means by which writers were able to distance themselves from the core of the action by presenting their work as either an ancient document, a story told second hand or by a series of diary entries or letters. The way in which Poe uses the newspaper articles is a variation of this, manipulated to enhance the overall effect and mystery of the text.

In interpreting this text and the other two Dupin stories as fundamentally Gothic then a little time must be spent analysing the range of characters within the text, specifically the role that Dupin himself holds as Gothic 'hero', or at the very least the way in which he can be perceived as a new breed of this conventional character. As with all Gothic victims Marie Rogêt, Madame and Mademoiselle L'Espanaye suffer at the hands of aggressors through no fault of their own, and Dupin's role as hero of the texts is to avenge the wrongs that have been done. When we move in to the realms of detective fiction there is of course a significant shift in the relationship between victim and hero, and that is that usually (unlike in traditional Gothic), the hero and the victim are unknown to each other and the interest that the 'hero' takes in the case is from an altogether outside perspective and motivated by profession, curiosity or intrigue.

Motivated by the solving of the mystery rather than a personal need to have the murderers of the victim brought to justice it can be seen that Dupin becomes a very different class of 'hero' than we have seen hereto. All the trimmings of fancy and emotional outbursts that one would expect were the hero to be directly involved in the case have been stripped away and consequently the remainder of the text is purely functional and linear in its presentation of logical surmises. It is this degree of removal of personal interest and association between the victims, heroes and villains that marks the most significant shift between conventional Gothic and this newly emerging Gothic-influenced detective fiction. At this early stage the detective genre it seems could not wholly function without the Gothic, but that is not to say that it was not able to manipulate the form for its own purposes.

In determining the Gothic influence on this early form of detective writing it would be wrong to assume that simply because the earliest detective stories bear the hallmark of the Gothic that all *subsequent* writing would also depend upon it for effect. To the contrary in the few years following Poe's Dupin stories the detective form began to grow and to develop independently and it became apparent that the Gothic trace was no longer a necessity when it came to writing a successful detective story.

Collins and Dickens: Grandfathers of Detective Fiction

Often hailed as the first true detective novel Wilkie Collins' *The Moonstone* (1868) demonstrates effectively the way in which the detective genre was able to operate independently and away from its Gothic roots, and Collins as a result of this has been credited with the ability to 'take the old-fashioned 'sensation' novel, strip it of its outmoded Gothic trimmings, and re-embody its essence in a Victorian domestic integument.'[81] With the exception of the original 'prophecy' regarding ownership of the Moonstone, this is indeed true; there is very little else that is any way reminiscent of the Gothic within the text.

The narrative focuses on a single mysterious event, the disappearance of a valuable diamond known as the Moonstone, shortly after it has been presented to Rachel Verinder as an eighteenth birthday present. Told from a number of different perspectives the novel mimics the way in which Poe infused a range of viewpoints and sources of information into his writing. By using a number of different narrators Collins is able to present the reader with a series of recollections each concerning the same event but coming from different sources. The reader becomes responsible for attempting to interpret the degrees of credibility in order to ascertain the facts of the diamond's disappearance before the final revelation at the end of the text. The result of this narrative technique is the introduction of a degree of gamesmanship or a battle of wits taking place between the reader and the author regarding the ability of the reader to solve the crime before the dénouement takes place, and is as much a feature of early detective fiction as it is today.

The other significant influence upon detective fiction of this period is of course Charles Dickens, and the impact that *he* had on the development of the genre and the influential role that he played in moving detective fiction even further away from its Gothic roots is an aspect that needs mentioning here. A contemporary of Collins, Dickens is often said to have been influenced by Collins, particularly Collins' use of first-person narrative, and there is scope to read his short novel *Hunted Down* (1859) as a story written 'in the manner of Wilkie Collins'[82]. *Hunted Down* is in many ways an interesting piece of writing, and one that Dickens was paid a huge sum of money to write. It is effectively a Newgate novel of sorts in that it depicts a poisoning and fraud that is widely believed to reflect the very real crimes committed by Thomas Wainewright and William Palmer.

However, whilst Collins and Dickens may have been contemporaries, there is much about their writing styles that differs and consequently, although both significant contributors to the development of detective fiction, they both brought something very different to the way in which the genre began to develop. Certainly Dickens can be credited as being among the first writers to develop a life and existence for his characters *outside* of the mystery of crime that the novel portrays. So often in early detective fiction characters exist solely for the purpose of linking them to the *crime* of the novel and they cease to become or to have any interest or function outside of that particular role. Such singularity of purpose is evident in Collins' *Moonstone* whereby despite the large number of characters within the text, they have no function other than to report their own perceptions and account of their movements at the time of the disappearance of the moonstone.

In many ways this simplicity of character in *The Moonstone* (and I mean of character, not of plot or of the mystery itself) is reminiscent of the one-dimensional characters found in first phase Gothic texts. Despite his reliability, humour and general affability, Betteridge has only one purpose in the text, and that is solely related to the main (and only) plot of novel that is the disappearance of the diamond. Dickens' writing by contrast is significantly more complex and often there are multiple plots at work and his characters are fully developed with histories, experiences and lives that are not always crucial to the main plot, whatever that might be.

Certainly Dickens' attention to detail is an aspect of his writing that sets him apart from so many of his contemporaries and so many other writers of early detective fiction, and this attention to detail is indeed evident in the 'wonderfully overpopulated' *Bleak House* (1853) whose characters are amongst the 'most vividly memorable'[83] of any in his texts. The novel is very much an example of early detective fiction, with Inspector Bucket occupying the role of the investigator, but has such intricacies of plot and so many characters that weave in an out of the main plot that it is easy to overlook this aspect to the novel. Like so many of Dickens' texts the main crime behind *Bleak House* is more to do with the failings of society as a whole rather than simply one specific crime. It is this that gives Dickens' work its strongest link to first phase Gothic writing that similarly demonstrated the failings of society that appeared to *demand* that crimes such as those carried out by Manfred of Walpole's *Otranto* be committed in order that the requirements of ancestry and heritage be met.

In *Bleak House* and also in *Great Expectations* society itself is portrayed as the real villain, the 'false patriarch'[84] in which its citizens are left to fend for themselves instead of being looked after by the 'authority that is supposed to nurture and protect them'[85], and it is this ability to look at the bigger picture so to speak that sets Dickens apart from almost every other writer of his day, Collins included. The inclusion of fully rounded characters, both investigators and criminals (a la Dickens) is very much a definitive part of modern crime fiction, and it is a technique used by many current writers as a means of generating sufficient scope and interest in the characters to sustain a series of novels that detail the activities of its central characters. Patricia Cornwell is one such writer to do this with great effect and the way in which she manages to do this successfully will be explored in Chapter 6 of this text.

Gothic and Detective Fiction Combined: Conan Doyle's *The Hound of the Baskervilles*

Whilst it is true that detective fiction was fast becoming a genre in its own right, there were writers who still relished the compatibility of the two genres and continued to use features of each to great effect. One of the most well known of these writers is Conan Doyle, whose 1901 *The Hound of the Baskervilles* serves as a perfect example of just how effectively the Gothic and detective fiction can combine to produce a chilling narrative.

By the time *The Hound of the Baskervilles* appeared in serial form in *The Strand Magazine*, Conan Doyle had already produced a great many Sherlock Holmes mysteries. The first novella to feature Holmes and Watson was *A Study in Scarlet* which appeared in 1887 in *Beeton's Christmas Annual,* and the pair of sleuths went on to feature in three more full-length novels and over 50 short stories, most of which appeared in *The Strand Magazine* between 1891 and 1893.

In 1893 Conan Doyle, seeming to have become somewhat fed up with the Holmes, produced a short story in which the amateur detective appeared to finally have met his doom. *The Final Problem,* which featured a violent struggle between Holmes and his arch enemy Professor Moriarty at Reichenbach Falls, strongly suggested that both of these characters had fallen to their deaths during the fight, and the reading public was reduced to wearing black armbands to demonstrate their grief at the death of this fictional hero. With neither body ever being found however, there was always the potential for Holmes to reappear at some stage, and in 1901 Holmes was reintroduced to the reading public in a nine-part serial entitled *The Hound of the Baskervilles.*

In the earlier much shorter mysteries Holmes, very much like Poe's

Dupin, promotes unspeakable logic, formidable deduction and the belief in reason above all else as a means of reaching the truth. In terms of theme, there is nothing supernatural about the short stories and indeed there is nothing traditionally Gothic within them either. The ultimate message of each is that there is always, no matter how seemingly bizarre or irrational the problem, a rational and logical explanation waiting to be found.

With this in mind it seems strange therefore, that Conan Doyle should re-introduce Holmes to the reading public with a novel such as *The Hound of the Baskervilles* in that it is a story so very different from its predecessors. Despite the fact that ultimately in the novel reason prevails over the super-natural and the mysterious hound is discovered to be an exceptionally large dog painted with a preparation of phosphorous (the sole objective of which being to frighten an old man to death for the purpose of inheritance), even Holmes, not usually one given to flights of emotional fancy, concedes that:

> In that gloomy tunnel it must indeed have been a dreadful sight to
> see that huge black creature, with its flaming jaws and blazing eyes,
> bounding after its victim.[86]

As the novel is primarily concerned with one character trying to engi-neer the inheritance of a house and its surrounding land, and on account of Sir Charles' belief 'that a dreadful fate overhung his family'[87] the novel's place as a Gothic text is entirely justified. Tie this in with the wonderfully atmospheric description of the sinister and remote Dartmoor setting ('in front of us rose the huge expanse of the moor, mottled with gnarled and craggy cairns and tors. A cold wind swept down from it and set us shiv-ering…It needed but this to complete the grim suggestiveness of the barren waste, the chilling wind and the darkling sky'[88]) and it becomes apparent that Conan Doyle is quite deliberately adopting Gothic motif and conven-tion within his writing.

Like a great many of its Gothic predecessors, the narrative of *The Hound of the Baskervilles* is largely composed of letters or diary entries made by Watson and sent back to Holmes in London whilst he supposedly remains there to finish work upon another case. As the novel draws towards its conclusion we realise however that this is not the case at all, and that instead of being in London, Holmes has in fact been hiding out upon the moor in an old stone hut in order to witness goings-on with suitable levels of both proximity and anonymity.

It is a very different type of detective narrative than was written by Poe in his heavily Gothic-influenced Dupin tales, and there is of course in this example a greater sense of conclusion and return to moral certainty than was seen in either the *Rue Morgue* or *Marie Rogêt*. Holmes is determined to solve the mystery, find the killer and restore some degree of order to the situation. Although Dr Mortimer is unknown to either Holmes or Watson at the beginning of the story, the fact that he approaches them so directly for help does establish a personal relationship between the characters that was absent from the Dupin texts. That is not to say that Holmes is at all motivated by the need to solve the mystery simply because he is acquainted with Dr Mortimer; like Dupin he is as always encouraged by the *prospect* of the challenge. But the extent to which Holmes forms opinions and judgments about Dr. Mortimer based upon the walking stick does bring to the text a greater sense of character and sentiment than was present in the somewhat cold and distant, purely professional, approach of Dupin.

By presenting such a large proportion of the text through the somewhat more personable eyes of Watson, Conan Doyle is able to bring a greater sense of humanity to his text than Poe did, and resultingly we are able to take greater interest in the characters and begin to care a great deal more for the outcome. Development of character was something that Collins did to great effect in *The Moonstone*, be it the perspective of the very likeable Gabriel Betteridge or the comical absurdity of Miss Clack, and this key element is of character development that is so much a part of traditional Gothic is notable in its absence from any of the Dupin mysteries.

By using Gothic setting and theme, and injecting these into a very traditional detective story (that is the logical presentation and following of clues combined with brilliant deduction and analytical ability), Conan Doyle has been able to demonstrate very effectively the ways in which these two genres can blend together for such dramatic effect.

The Rise of Detective Fiction: Golden Age versus Hard Boiled

By the late 1800s detective writing in Britain had truly taken shape and established itself as a genre in its own right. The introduction of Conan Doyle's Sherlock Holmes in 1887 heralded a spree of detective writing that culminated in England with the Golden Age period of between 1920 and 1939. Often labelled as classic detective fiction, novels produced in this period are typically gentle in tone with very little emphasis or detail upon the brutality or savageness of the crime and in this respect differ greatly from the heavily Gothicised work of Poe. Agatha Christie, Dorothy Sayers,

Freeman Wills Crofts and Anthony Berkeley Cox were among the most noted of these Golden Age writers and their work is characterised by a clear set of principles and an element of fair play to the mystery whereby following the clues and paying attention to detail, the reader should have a fair shot at solving the mystery before the final denouement or big 'reveal'. In these stories logic and analysis prevail, but not to the extent of work by Poe or Conan Doyle in which it is almost impossible for the reader to solve the mystery and there is no sense of fair game.

Produced in their masses in the years following the First World War these classic novels differ greatly from the bleakness and gloom associated with many of Dickens' text and certainly seemed to offer a degree of stability and predictability, possessing strong moral cores that are notably absent from earlier examples of detective fiction. The morality and decency that these Golden Age texts portray is of course understandable and appropriate if we are looking to historical context as a means of understanding and accounting for the popularity and allure of certain genres. However, this emphasis on stability and moral righteousness has often led to criticism of Golden Age writing, highlighting as it does the propensity for conservatism and lack of realism that such dependency on 'putting things right' inevitably causes. There are of course obvious advantages and a degree of pleasantry associated with a genre that was so ready and willing to bring both 'social stability and moral certainty'[89] to a world which had neither at the time.

It is widely accepted that the primary purpose of the detective novel of this post-war period was the 'restoring [of] the social and moral status quo'[90] within the chaos of the era in which they were written, and that consequently texts of this period absolutely and deliberately excluded 'situations and characters which posed ethically defensible opposition to established values.'[91] The result may have been a more 'secure' reading experience for the reader, but at what cost was this security? Certainly there is some truth in the suggestion that by adhering so rigidly to such strict moral guidelines authors of this particular form of detective fiction 'bound themselves to a narrow and perhaps narrow-minded view of English society'[92]

In terms of plot and structure these Golden Age novels are easier to describe in general terms than to offer exacting definition of how each individual story unfolds, as they do adhere to a set of conventions and features that are just as rigid and predictable as the 'ingredients' were to the Gothic genre. Often in the Golden Age novel there is a rural location; a village or a country house, a very limited circle of suspects, one or maybe two corpses – perhaps poisoned or shot, maybe with a single stab wound (certainly there would be no glorification over the body or the mode of death) and a big reveal at the end of the text where the exposé of the culprit would occur in a grand finale and finger-pointing showdown in front of all of the characters in the text and would generate surprise for the reader only if they had failed to follow the clues and identify the felon before the moment of dénouement.

Of course the code of convention that these novels adhered to was reminiscent of the formulaic approach of the Gothic, but otherwise they bear little resemblance to Gothic texts. By this period in time detective fiction had branched away entirely from its Gothic forefather and there was seldom any evidence that the two had ever been related.

In order to prove this point and therefore advocate the independent nature of detective writing, the Catholic priest Ronald Knox in 1929 established a set of 'Ten Commandments' that seemed intentionally to separate detective fiction from other literary genres. In attempting to distance the detective genre specifically away from the Gothic, Knox stated that within detective writing 'all supernatural and preternatural agencies are ruled out as a matter of course' and that 'not more than one secret room or passage is allowable.'[93] The result of these 'commandments' and other lists similar to them was the ultimate recognition that detective fiction was beholden to the Gothic no more, and that instead it was to be regarded as an established genre in its own right.

With such specific focus on the polite reserve of the English middle and upper classes, the Golden Age of detective fiction was for the most part a British movement, and although there were very successful American writers of this type of detective fiction (S. S. Van Dine, Ellery Queen and John Dickson Carr are among the better known and most prominent of these) American detective fiction is most strongly associated with the hard-boiled style of writing as produced in great volume by writers such as Dashiell Hammett and Carroll John Daly in the 1920s. The most well known writers of this hard-boiled form of the genre began writing and publishing their stories in the American pulp magazine *Black Mask*. Both Hammett and Daly were early contributors to this magazine and later the magazine also provided the stepping stone for Raymond Chandler, Erle Stanley Gardner and Paul Cain to launch their literary careers.

In the same way as British and American Gothic differed so greatly, so too did British and American detective fiction. Radically different from the Golden Age style, hard-boiled detective fiction is always much darker in tone, with much greater emphasis on violence and brutality. The niceties of the British form of the genre (country manors, afternoon teas and afternoon walks) are replaced with a much greater sense of gritty realism as private eyes reject pleasantry and comfort in favour of simply telling it like it is; they drink and smoke heavily, carry guns and are not afraid to use them, fight and generally manage to scrape a living for themselves by removing lowlifes from the streets of America's toughest cities.

Despite being so different from Golden Age detective fiction, the hard-boiled form of the genre is just as affected by form and convention at its British equivalent, and perhaps surprisingly, *its* code of convention gives it just as much predictability and cliché as the British form. Appearing most prolifically in the same period as British Golden Age fiction (emerging in the years following the First World War up until the late 1930s) it seems also that the rise of hard-boiled fiction owes as much to its post-war social, political and economic context as the Golden Age school did to its own set of circumstances. There is huge propensity for this type of fiction to concentrate on the 'experiential divide' between 'stable, predictable patterns and the recognition that life is, in truth, morally chaotic, subject to randomness and total dislocation'[94] and just as Golden Age detective fiction was born in response to its context so too was hard-boiled writing, with 'the impetus [coming] from the conditions of American life and the opportunities available to the American writer in the 1920s.'[95] Certainly there is evidence to support the belief that 'the economic boom following the First World War combined with the introduction of the Prohibition in 1920 to encourage the rise of the gangster...It took no great leap of imagination for them [the authors] to tackle modern crime and detection, fresh from the newspaper headlines of the day, and create heroes with the same vigour as their well-established favourites.'[96]

If we are to understand and accept that much of the gentle predictability of Golden Age writing represents an attempt to offer stability and a sense of grounding to a shaken nation and to offer some degree of comfort and reassurance to its readers, we can see that writers of hard-boiled fiction were motivated by something very different. With a much greater sense of gritty reality and distinctly darker in tone, American hard-boiled detective fiction is very rarely a 'pleasant' read and the deeper undercurrents and sense of insecurity that run throughout these novels are rarely resolved once the original mystery has been solved. Instead they give the feeling that the problem that has been solved is small scale in comparison to the greater wrongs that are at work within society as a whole.

In Britain the Golden Age form of writing continued to appear in the years during and after the Second World War, and Agatha Christie in particular continued writing until well into the 1970s. In America however another dramatic shift in the genre occurred and detective fiction began to move away from the concept of crime-ridden cities, bar brawls and flawed PIs. In the 1950s a new genre emerged – one that still had the concept of detection at its core, but that demonstrated increasing reliance upon the psychology of criminals and their crimes in a manner more associated with the Gothic writings of Lewis and Radcliffe and latterly Shelley and Poe also. It is this fusion of psychological Gothic with detection that forms the basis for the beginnings of modern crime fiction, a genre that began to emerge in the 1950s in America and appeared in Britain in the early 1960s. Amongst the earliest examples of modern crime fiction are British author John Fowles' *The Collector* (1963) and also Robert Bloch's novel *Psycho* (1959), both of which showcase the features of the newly emerging genre perfectly. It is to Bloch's novel however, that this book shall turn next, providing as it does an excellent example of the ways in which the Gothic and detective genre combine to produce an altogether different form of writing.

CHAPTER THREE

Understanding a Nation's Fear: Distrust and Devolution in Robert Bloch's *Psycho*

O N E of the first novels to successfully combine traditional Gothic with a detective led theme was Robert Bloch's 1959 novel *Psycho*. In this very early example of modern crime fiction it is the search for the missing Mary Crane that forms much of the main plot and becomes the detection aspect of the novel, and the sinister presence of Mother Bates and the Bates house that encapsulate the Gothic theme. If we are to accept modern crime fiction as being composed of these two elements, then it should be easy to recognise *this* particular text as being an early example of this newly emerging genre.

Having been described as being one of the 'most powerful'[97] of all twentieth-century horror myths, there is no doubting the fact that Robert Bloch's *Psycho* is a great modern classic text, combining as it does elements of the Gothic and detective fiction (that lean more towards the hard-boiled school of writing than to golden age form), with a great sense of paranoia and persecution that is very much representative of its own social and political context. Largely overshadowed by the success of Alfred Hitchcock's 1960 film interpretation of the text, the fact that the story originates from a novel is often overlooked. It is on the novel itself rather than the film (although certain aspects of the film will be touched upon) that this chapter intends to focus.

Early Gothic Influence

When reading the text it is easy to recognise the elements of the Gothic that Bloch has drawn upon. First and foremost we have perhaps to consider the plot itself, and the way in which that can be defined as Gothic. Essentially the narrative focuses on the disappearance (murder) of Mary Crane and the attempts made by the deranged Norman Bates to cover it up from the interrogations and questions posed by Arbogast, Loomis and Mary's sister, Lila. Much of the narrative, as is so often typical of the Gothic, is driven by secrecy and secrets that, despite the desires of the perpetrator to remain hidden, have a nasty way of coming to light.

With the exception of the scenes that take place in Loomis' hardware store, the novel is almost entirely set either in the Bates' motel or in the Bates' family home that lies atop of the hill behind the motel, and it is the latter of the two that is perhaps the most traditionally Gothic in its description:

> The house was old, its frame siding gray and ugly here in the half-light
> of the coming storm. Porch boards creaked under her feet, and she could
> hear the wind rattling the casements of the upstairs windows.[98]

Were this description of a semi-ruinous house not quite enough, we have also to remember that it comes complete with cellar and shrivelled corpse to boot.

Another Gothic feature that Bloch makes heavy use of is the presence of gloomy weather and the ominous atmosphere that it creates to generate a sense of suspense within the text. Typically in the Gothic the weather (specifically bad weather) acts as a form of early warning system for the onset of danger or peril, and this device is one that Shelley makes great use of in *Frankenstein* as the monster is brought to life during the most savage and primitive of thunder storms. In *Psycho* this technique is evident within the narrative from the very outset of the novel as Norman is shocked by the sudden sound of rain beating against the parlour window, presenting the reader with the rather eerie image of the sound being like that of somebody 'tapping on the window pane'[99]. Certainly this level of suspense is maintained through the rapid pace of the novel as Bloch on more than one occasion uses the interjection of this form of pathos into the text as a means of engaging with the reader's emotions and manipulating the way in which we respond to the text.

It is certainly an effective technique, and one that has been used time and time again by authors of all genres and from all periods in history. Indeed the effect that this stylistic technique can have on a text is demonstrable; think only of the dramatic and memorable introduction to *Great Expectations* to understand how this works. In this example we are presented with the image of the young boy Pip alone, afraid and crying in the graveyard beyond which lie the sinister and terrifying marshes:

...infant children...were also dead and buried...the dark, flat wilderness
beyond the churchyard, intersected with dykes and mounds and gates...
was the marshes...the distant savage lair from which the wind was
rushing, was the sea...the small bundle of shivers growing afraid of it all
and beginning to cry, was Pip.[100]

Certainly this dramatic build up of atmosphere and tension hints
strongly at the impending danger that the convict poses to Pip. Consider
also the ways in which the sudden onset of rolling mists and sweeping frets
in Susan Hill's *The Woman in Black* contribute so enormously to the feelings
of suspense and unease that pervade the novel. The mists (accompanied as
they are) by the sound of the pony trap and harrowing screams hint strongly
at a past tragedy and an awful secret that is waiting to be revealed. When
used in the right hands this stylistic device becomes a very powerful tool
and it is certainly not without effect in *Psycho*, as is evident in the dramatic
claps of thunder that accompany Lila as she descends the steps to the cellar
just before she makes the horrific discovery of Mother Bates' mummified
corpse:

The basement stairs were just ahead. She fumbled at the wall until
her hand brushed over another switch. The light went on below, just a
faint and faltering glow in the darkened depths. Thunder growled in
counterpoint to the clatter of her heels.[101]

It would be a mistake however, to assume that Bloch has merely drawn
on perhaps the most obvious aspects of the Gothic and employed them
cheaply as a means of giving Gothic validation to his novel. On the contrary,
he has chosen them with precision as a means of generating deeper meaning
within his work, raising it far above mere page-turning paperback thriller.
Those aspects of the Gothic that he has chosen to employ have been carefully selected and each are worthy of serious critical analysis. Perhaps the
most obvious of these Gothic trappings is the motel and the house that
form the primary locations for much of the narrative. I have already briefly
touched upon the Gothic atmosphere that surround the house in particular,
but more importantly these two locations are significant when it comes to
understanding the complex divide and overlap of personalities at work
within Bates himself. Critical analysis has in the past given much credence
to the concept that Gothic settings have much greater symbolic and metaphoric value than mere bricks and mortar, and *Psycho* is no exception.

The Significance of Structure

In order to explain this more fully, it is necessary for a moment return to Walpole's *Otranto*, specifically Isabella's flight from the lustful Manfred, to see how indeed the physical aspect of Manfred's home, the castle itself, ceases to hold importance as merely a building, but becomes instead representative of something much more sinister. It is whilst trying to escape Manfred, that Isabella opts for an escape route that takes her into the innermost parts of the castle, through a network of subterranean passages and vaults that as well as providing the perfect Gothic setting, become in themselves representative of the innermost recesses of Manfred's mind. Dark and twisted pathways become a physical manifestation of the darker side to Manfred's character and to this extent Manfred literally *is* the castle; multi-layered and altogether dangerous. When Conrad dies its very existence is threatened; no son to continue the family line and the family will collapse, which is of course what happens physically (the collapse of the castle) and symbolically (the end of Manfred's lineage) at the end of the text when Manfred fails in his pursuit of Isabella.

This same duality of purpose is also evident in the role that the house holds in Poe's *The Fall of the House of Usher* (1839) where again the central theme of the text is the desperate need of the head of house, Roderick Usher, to beget a male heir and thus guarantee and preserve the future lineage of the 'House'. Interestingly in this example, the link between house and self is much more explicit, and it becomes evident from very early on in the text that Roderick and the House physical are indeed one and that their existences cannot be separated or analysed independently of one another. Poe's use of ominous weather is certainly fanciful and perhaps lacking in subtlety, but it serves to demonstrate the relationship between the house and Roderick perfectly:

> Its evidence – the evidence of the sentience – was to be seen, he said, (and here I started as he spoke,) in the gradual yet certain condensation of an atmosphere of their own about the waters and the walls. The result was discoverable, he added, in that silent, yet importunate and terrible influence which for centuries had moulded the destinies of his family, and which made *him* what I now saw him – what he was.[102]

Again, we can see the union that is created between the patriarch of the house, and the house itself. Upon Roderick's death the 'House of Usher' that is the future of the family name and destiny ceases to exist, and the house must metaphorically and physically fall, which it does, just as it did in *Otranto*.

How, though can we use this example of Gothic writing by Poe to extract meaning from Bloch's text and what does it tell us about the symbolic or metaphoric nature of modern crime fiction? Does this have any relevance to the ways in which we might interpret *Psycho* and understand the role that it occupies as a Gothic-influenced text? In order to answer these questions, let us turn back to the novel itself and play closer attention to the two structures that dominate the text, the house and the motel, as a means of understanding the role that they each play in reflecting Norman's state of mind.

Firstly and importantly, the motel is Norman's domain. It is the place where he operates and manages himself publicly on a day-to-day basis. In terms of psychological meaning the motel in this respect becomes representative of the conscious part of Norman's mind; that part of his that is able to function, albeit a little oddly, as Norman Bates, a shy, introspective, fat and bespectacled man approaching middle age. Within the confines of the motel itself, Bates' identity is relatively simple and he is free to be himself and to indulge himself in his hobbies and that which interests him; taxidermy, alcohol and playing peeping tom. It is only when he removes himself from this environment, and takes himself back into the house that problems begin and conflict emerges.

Certainly the far more dangerous and far more volatile environment for Norman is the house itself, set back from the motel, alone and brooding on the hill top. Just as it did in both *Otranto* and *The Fall of the House of Usher*, the house in *Psycho* becomes symbolic of the subconscious mind, that part of ourselves and of Norman that is private, secret and out of reach of anyone else. It is the conduit and the metaphor that allows us as reader access to subconscious thoughts and feelings that we otherwise would not have, and it is this concept of privacy and secrecy that is crucial in understanding the chain of events that form the narrative direction of the novel.

Whereas the motel is exclusively Norman's domain, understanding ownership of the house is a little more complicated. Throughout the text we are led to believe that it is Norman's mother who holds the dominant position in the house, and that Norman when he enters the house adopts a significantly more subservient role than that which he holds when he is in the motel. A simple assumption for the reader to make no doubt, but certainly an aspect of the text that takes on greater significance and psychological complexity when we realise that Mother Bates physically, at least, is dead and in fact only continues to 'live' in Norman's mind. When Norman returns to the house he is able to indulge in that part of himself, that private and inner space in his mind where his identity is compromised. Consequently he begins to incorporate his mother's persona into his own, giving rise to a division of identity or a multiple personality disorder. The splits in Norman's identity are physically represented within the narrative as two entirely separate structures or domains, and the confusion and initial crime that takes place in the text (the murder of Mary Crane), results from the blurring of boundaries between these two separate identities and the two halves of Bates' mind that consequently begin to overlap.

As Mary is invited up to the house for supper so she moves from the open and public *conscious* part of Norman's mind into the more sinister and private *subconscious* place that is reserved for and largely dominated by Mother. As the narrative moves from the motel to the house, the subconscious (Mother) is forced out of its dormant state and made to confront the reality (Norman and Mary) of the conscious state and this is a confrontation that it does not understand and devolution occurs between these two precariously balanced emotional worlds. The object of the confusion is Mary herself representing as she does a link between these two opposing worlds that should never meet. It is when they do meet, and overlap between the public and the private occurs, that there are dramatic repercussions.

Normal order (that is the 'normal' state of affairs for Bates) is suspended as these two worlds collide; metaphorically speaking black has mixed with white and an intermediary grey that links and confuses the two has been created. In order for harmony to be restored between the two halves, the object of confusion (Mary) must be removed. Cue the infamous shower scene and the problem is resolved; Bates and his mother can resume their co-existence within the darker recesses of Bates' mind, at least until the arrival of Arbogast throws another spanner in the works, threatening as it does to undermine once again the delicately balanced relationship between the 'inner' and the 'outer' aspects of Bates family life.

Norman Bates: A 'Fragmented Personality'?

When thinking of traditional Gothic characters, it is the aggressive and forceful males, the marginalised females and the young hero that spring readily to mind. Interestingly Bloch chooses only to adhere to a few of these conventions and offers instead a significantly different alternative to the male-dominated structure that we associated with traditional Gothic writing. In an interesting alternative to conventional Gothic form the range of characters that we find in Bloch's novel reject the strong patriarchal hierarchy that typifies the early gothic phase and instead introduces an apparent reversal of roles whereby the dominancy of *this* text is demonstrably female and as a result of this the male characters in the novel, having been stripped of all force and power, become, to all extents and purposes, impotent.

Certainly Norman himself holds no strong masculine qualities in the text. Quite the opposite in fact he is very much presented as a rather pathetic figure, embarrassed and ill at ease in the presence of female company that is not Mother (although towards the end of the text as his identity becomes more confused he becomes increasingly uncomfortable and less sure with regard his 'relationship' with her too). His seeming reluctance to sever the apron strings as it were is something that Mary Crane notices immediately and indeed makes comment on:

> Mr. Bates, you'll pardon me for saying this but how long do you intend
> to go on this way? You're a grown man. You certainly must realize that
> you can't be expected to act like a little boy all the rest of your life. I don't
> mean to be rude, but –[103]

In this respect, Norman for the most part demonstrates many of those characteristics that we have come to recognise as being weak and passively aggressive in nature, those most strongly associated with the weaker, subservient female characters of early Gothic writing. He is not strong enough to stand up to 'Mother', but certainly when provoked by Mary he reveals an innate unexplored and unmanageable rage that has hereto has been a hidden aspect of Bates' persona :

> The voice wasn't soft and apologetic any longer; it was high and shrill.
> And the pudgy man was on his feet, his hands sweeping a cup from the
> table. It shattered on the floor, but Mary didn't look at it...[104]

It is interesting that Norman appears to interpret Mary's words as an attack on *Mother* rather than as a comment about *himself* as regards to the very oddness of the situation that is presented within the text. Certainly Mary's suggestion that Norman might consider an institution for Mother is perceived and taken as a direct threat towards Mother, and in his rush to defend and to protect her, Norman's dormant rage is spiked and it is at this point that the reader is given their first glimpse into the unstable nature of his character. Indeed Norman's mental make-up is a complex issue to address and understanding the complexities at work within his mind is never going to be wholly scientific; there is no one theory that can account for its psychology entirely successfully.

One of the more interesting theories that relates to Norman's identity issues makes much use of the concept of blurred boundaries within the text, suggesting that the blurring that occurs is indicative of 'fragmentation' occurring within Norman's mind. The assertion that Norman's mind is 'fragmented' with evidence of 'splitting' and that the story itself is less one 'of the disintegration of a personality than one of a massive attempt by the psyche to *reseal* itself'[105] is indeed interesting, and one that certainly warrants attention in terms of determining its accuracy.

By definition fragmentation refers to the breaking down into smaller pieces of a particular subject or object that at some prior point in time was whole. It seems within the text itself however, that those characters that occupy Norman's mind space (his own and that of Mother) rather than being 'fragmented' are instead absolutely rounded, whole and complete personalities complexly conjoined and battling within the one physical mind space that is Norman's brain. It would appear that rather than arising from *fragmentation* of a personality or personalities, Norman's troubles result from the very *accumulation* of complete characters within his mind. Certainly one of the central themes to *Psycho* seems to be Bloch's ongoing exploration into the psychological capacity of man, querying the level to which we can successfully operate and exist once our individuality (or oneness) is compromised.

Norman's mental collapse or devolution is a direct result of the upset caused by Mary Crane of the very precarious balance between the two personalities that his mind is having to support. There is no fragmentation, rather it is the increasing instability of whole personas within him that occurs when one of his personalities, that of Mother, begins to take on a more dominant role and begins to be able to operate in both the subconscious and the conscious areas of Norman's mind.

Rather than being a story of 'disintegration' or of 'fragmentation', *Psycho* appears to be a tale of devolution of character or characters. In order to cope both with grief, loss and guilt, Norman's mind has evolved in such a complex and confused manner that he has effectively given re-birth to his mother, brought her back to life and allowed her to continue to live within himself so that he can continue to exist. Thus the novel becomes more of a tale of re-affirmation of the bond between Norman and his Mother than an attempt by the mind to 'reseal' itself and Norman's devolution, or collapse, occurs when this mother/child bond is interrupted by the arrival of Mary Crane.

Norman's dependency upon Mother, his simultaneous loving and loathing of her, prevent him from ever being able to function without her and it is the realisation of this that forces him to find an alternative means of 'living' with her once he has killed her. By living alongside her corpse and giving her space within his own mind he fosters a degree of nurture and protection over Mother that he simply did not have, or was not permitted to have whilst she was alive. Effectively what we have as a result is a reversal or inversion of the mother/child bond whereby Mrs Bates occupies an alternative 'in utero' role within Norman's mind. Certainly Norman's actions are the result of the need to appease his guilt over his mother's death, but they occur also as a result of a much more fundamental and basic survival instinct; realising that he simply cannot survive without her, it becomes necessary to fashion an alternative existence whereby he *can* live with her in some shape or form. He may be looking for a solution for his problem, but this is not necessarily akin to the 'resealing' of himself.

Devolution, not disintegration, occurs when evolvement (that is the growth of the characters within his mind) has reached saturation point. 'Mother' has been allowed to grow and to develop and is no longer a force that can be restrained by Norman, and this is why the concept of *re*sealing is not wholly accurate, in that there is nothing sealed about the forces at work within Norman's mind or indeed the environment in which we find him in the first place. There is no harmony between the voices in his head, no equilibrium betwixt them as each battle to have his or her voice heard above the other. Each character is constantly changing and growing at the expense of another, depending on where the action of the story is set at that particular time (the house or the motel). The joint existence between the characters of Bates and Mother is in no way hermetically sealed, instead it is open to external influence (Mary, Arbogast, Loomis and Lila) that constantly threatens to undermine it.

Stevenson's *Jekyll and Hyde*: An Early Example of Devolution

If we are to accept *Psycho* as having roots firmly placed in the Gothic, then certainly the concept of multiple personality is one that warrants further attention, reminiscent as it is in so many ways of the battle between personalities that forms the central theme to Robert Louis Stevenson's *The Strange Case of Dr Jekyll and Mr Hyde*. First published in 1886, *Jekyll and Hyde* is largely focused on the mysterious existence of the rather sinister Mr Hyde and his curious relationship to the much more benevolent but reclusive Dr Jekyll. The tale has a somewhat modern Gothic setting in London where the luxuries and genteelness of the upper classes are undermined by a mysterious and violent character that stalks the night instilling terror in those who come across him. Due to the covert nature of Hyde's existence, much of the narrative takes place at night, under the cover of darkness and there is of course no subtlety in the employment of this aspect of Gothic traditionalism whereby monsters quite literally are lurking in the deepest shadows.

The most interesting aspect of this particular example of Gothic writing however is the way in which Stevenson explores the concept of conscious and the subconscious forces at work within us, and it is this that forms the strongest link between this text and *Psycho*. It is not until the final chapter of the book that we finally are permitted to hear Dr Jekyll's account of the events that appear to have befallen him, for the rest of the book is largely made up of the observations of Mr Utterson and the hearsay that he is privy to. It is only at length then that we become aware of Jekyll's belief that all men harbour within them a subconscious identity, a second self if you like that remains hidden away, constantly forced to repress its urges and desires by the more morally sound 'public' face. Jekyll's belief that 'man is not truly one, but truly two'[106] and his subsequent attempts and doomed success in separating these two identities are ultimately his downfall as he releases a force within himself that his 'good' side cannot contain or control and he finds himself becoming easy victim for the stronger and predatory Hyde.

But how exactly is this relevant to our understanding of *Psycho*? One of the most compelling aspects of each of these tales is the ultimate consumption of the 'public' identity by the stronger subconscious 'private' force (devolution) and the exposure of the untapped evil potential of the human mind that the process reveals. Evidently both *Jekyll and Hyde* and *Psycho* appear to carry the message that by giving in to this aspect of yourself and letting your innermost thoughts and desires out, you are in effect sealing your own fate as there is no competition between our public selves and the sheer dominance of force of the subconscious once we breathe life into it and permit it to begin to grow within us. Of course there is much to be said about the extent to which we are responsible for allowing this to happen. Certainly for Norman there appears to have been little choice; consumed with guilt and sorrow his subconscious seems to have sought out the best way to protect itself, and consequently exactly how much Norman is to blame for his own very complicated state of mind is debatable. The same cannot be said for Henry Jekyll however, who has brought about his own downfall by indulging in perhaps ill-thought-out experimentation whereby the true ramifications of separating the 'polar twins'[107] housed within our minds were simply not given enough respect. Henry Jekyll's arrogance and blindness is very much reminiscent of those flaws within Victor Frankenstein who similarly brought about his own ruin and the ruin of very many others in the wake of *his* ill-conceived scientific experimentation.

Certainly this focus on the evil nature and duality of forces at work within us is a significant step away from the role that the supernatural played in the very earliest examples of Gothic fiction. There is nothing at work in either *Jekyll and Hyde* or *Psycho* that suggest even for a minute that the horrors that unfold in each of the stories are related to anything other than the curse of mankind to be in possession of a brain and of a mind more latently powerful than anyone has given it credit for. Whether we live in a society that is strongly religious or not, demonstrably the evil that mankind harbours within himself and is capable of and the terror that he can inflict of both himself and those around him is, for the modern reader, an altogether more terrifying prospect than ghostly goings-on.

Jekyll and Hyde, like many of its early Gothic forerunners is a text that is very much patriarchal and male-dominated in its structure. Without exception each of the principal characters are not only male, but also they are *successful* men, unpretentious and well-meaning persons whose moral soundness and respectability form a crucial part in giving authenticity to the text. In moving the genre as a whole away from the explicitly sensational and over the top dramatic plot lines of the early Gothic, the introduction of characters such as Utterson helps to produce a story that is not only more sure footed and mature in tone but more credible also.

Indeed there is a strong air of realism within Stevenson's story, and his skilful handling of both character and setting generate a plausibility to the text whereby the reader can speculate just a little as to how such a series of events might actually unfold. The text appeared in the wake of much scientific and medicinal discovery and resultingly the story is nicely poised against this backdrop of progress and change. *Psycho* too is not without cultural context and significance, and this aspect of the text will be explored in greater detail when we come to examine the detective aspect to the text.

There is however a stark contrast between this text and Bloch's *Psycho* that is revealed when we begin to look at the way in which these two texts are structured in relation to the way in which gender stereotypes are applied. *Jekyll and Hyde* is arguably a text in which females are significantly marginalised, and there are several reasons for this. The first is possibly a part of Stevenson remaining true to the traditional Gothic form that promotes patriarchal strength and dominance, despite the misadventure that it causes, and secondly it is, as I have already touched on, a means of giving authenticity to the tale.

Stevenson's men are articulate, specific, reliable witnesses not given to flights of fancy or whimsy; their accounts are not only to be believed, but they are also to be taken seriously. Stevenson makes his point in detailing the specific differences between the two sexes when he gives his only female speaking part the chance to recount her witness of the Carew Murder Case as reported by the narrator:

> It seems that she was romantically given; for she sat down upon her box, which stood immediately under the window, and fell into a dream of musing...She became aware of an aged and beautiful gentleman with white hair drawing along the lane...the moon shone as he spoke, and the girl was pleased to watch it, it seemed to breathe such an innocent and old-world kindness of disposition...[108]

Were this description not enough to demonstrate to us the sentimental nature of the seemingly fairer sex, Stevenson ensures that we are suitably aware of the fragility and emotional disposition of womankind as he recounts that the maid, upon witnessing the savagery of the attack that befalls Sir Danvers, 'fainted'[109].

Although it is a statement to be trusted, and there is no suggestion that the maid is in anyway telling an untruth, what this quote demonstrates is the female capacity to be predisposed to fanciful imagination and an inability to confront abject horror that in turn renders the account unreliable in that the attention is taken away from the actual attack on Sir Danvers itself and placed instead upon the maid and her well-being. That she fainted delayed the arrival of the police by some two hours, by which point any chance to apprehend the murderer *in situ* had been lost.

Lest the momentum and direction of the text be lost, what Stevenson then gives us is a strong and reliable *male* narrator to guide us through the plot, focusing on and giving us only that information that is imperative to our understanding of the text as a whole. Certainly Mr Utterson's clinical and somewhat austere description of Mr Hyde provides a stark contrast to the somewhat romantic and whimsical nature of the maid's observations. By contrast Utterson's words are measured and controlled, conveying the pride and responsibility that Utterson takes upon himself to deliver a testimony that is concise and accurate – we can compare the maid's account already quoted with that of Utterson:

...he began slowly to mount the street, pausing every step or two, and putting his hand to his brow like a man in perplexity...Mr Hyde was pale and dwarfish; he gave the impression of deformity without any nameable malformation, he had a displeasing smile, he had borne himself to the lawyer with a sort of murderous mix of timidity and boldness, and he spoke with husky whispering and somewhat broken voice, – all these were points against him, but not all of these together could explain the hitherto unknown disgust, loathing and fear with which Mr Utterson regarded him.[110]

It is obvious within the text that the onus of the investigation and the ultimate solving of the peculiar mystery that revolves around Henry Jekyll has been placed upon this reliable and respected man, and it is to his credit that he is able to draw upon the opinions and expertise of his like-minded *male* friends and colleagues in order to do this successfully and effectively.

It is interesting when we make the comparison between the two texts then, to find that this strong and reliable male-dominated environment is a concept that Bloch rejects outright. There is very much a sense of inversion within his text of the typical gender roles as we see male prowess and ability replaced with widespread impotence and a trio of female characters that dominate and control both the main plot and the sub-plot.

Let us start by examining the role played by Norman himself, and explore the level of control that he has in forming and shaping his own character and destiny within the story. To all intents and purposes Norman is presented as a weak, effeminate middle-aged man who still lives with his mother. He is ill at ease around Mary, blushes easily and seems embarrassed when confronted with her sexuality and the contrast with his own lack of sexual experience. It is not that Norman is without sexual interest, we know as much from his voyeuristic enterprises with the office wall peephole, it is just that he has no capacity for gaining normal experience living as closely as he does within the confines of Mother's control.

He has no prowess, no charm or allure for women and is not intimidating or frightening in the least. Indeed it is his inoffensive and seemingly harmless appearance that convinces Mary that there is nothing threatening or criminal about this man and to stay at the Motel in the first place, making up her mind as she does 'very quickly, once she saw the fat, bespectacled face and heard the soft, hesitant voice'[111]. Ultimately she pays with her life for her perhaps innocent mistake in deducing that 'there wouldn't be any trouble'[112] as she ignores the old cliché that the quiet ones are the worst.

Perkins as Bates: A New Breed of Monster

Having detailed the way in which Bates' character is portrayed in the text it is interesting to consider Hitchcock's representation of Norman Bates in his 1960 interpretation of the text. Interestingly the role was cast to Anthony Perkins, a considerably more 'manly' specimen than was originally intended by Bloch. Whereas Bloch's Bates is overweight, frumpy and markedly effeminate, Perkins is very much the opposite. Tall, dark and handsome he is a far cry from Bloch's pathetic character. Indeed the first time we meet him in the film, as Mary Crane arrives at the Motel, we are confronted with a charming and witty conversationalist, with an air of confidence and a definite sex appeal, to whom Janet Leigh's Mary is attracted.

At the dinner scene there is only the faintest echo of Bloch's original character present. Whilst it is true that Perkins' Bates is awkward in Mary's company; he stutters and stammers through much of the meal, he also comes across as very articulate and insightful. He is evidently an emotional man, dutiful with regards to caring for his mother, but there is also a tangible air of sinister menace and deliberate calculation to Perkin's Bates that was not present in Bloch's text. That the two Norman's are so very different simply cannot be ignored; why did Hitchcock feel it was necessary to make such a change away from the original text, and what did he believe that the film would stand to gain from such a change?

In order to answer this, we need to consider what the film was trying to achieve. Certainly box office success was the chief motivation, but is there anything else that the film is trying to do that the book could not? Arguably the principal genre of the *film* is horror, and the success of this depends entirely on the credibility of the levels of suspense that are generated within it. Without a doubt, creating and maintaining suspense successfully is Hitchcock's forte; he does it masterfully with every aspect of his film from the instantly recognisable music to the absolute precision with which each scene is shot.

With this in mind it begs the question could the same effect have been achieved if Hitchcock had stayed true to the original Bates and chosen someone less striking to play the role? The answer to this is almost certainly no. Almost definitely the film would have lost much of its suspense if the lead role was taken by an overweight and unattractive American failure. What makes Perkins so effective is that both physically and visibly he represents a successful all-round American guy. He is attractive, charming and successful; caring in the dutiful attention he gives to his poor, sick mother and certainly someone to whom ladies are attracted.

Superficially at least he is the type of guy men want to be like and women want to spend time with. That he is revealed to be so deeply troubled is all the more shocking for this. Who, after all would be so very surprised that Bloch's somewhat pathetic character should turn out to be such a, well, psycho? But that Perkins should be one? Well that's altogether a much more sinister thought. If Perkins can be so dangerous underneath all that seeming prowess, then quite possibly *anyone* can, and that thought alone is surely enough to make you want to sleep with the lights on.

By casting Perkins as Bates, Hitchcock was able to restore some degree of power to the male gender, but this was never the intention in the book. To weaken the male species and invert traditional Gothic form by shifting the power from the male to the female is both a deliberate and a conscious decision by Bloch, and in the text we find that whereas Norman, Loomis and to a certain extent Arbogast fail to exert control over the direction of the text, it is the female characters of Mother Bates, Mary and her sister Lila who shun the traditional roles of submissive female and assume total power and domination within it.

Bloch's Dominant Women

Of these female characters the one that sets the ball rolling, so to speak is of course Mary Crane. Despite the fact that her physical role is the text is short lived, it is the mystery regarding her disappearance that pushes the story forward. We have already established the role that Mary plays as a go-between between the public and the private spaces of Norman's mind, and we have evaluated the damning consequences that occur when these two parts collide, but what we have not done is assess the role that Mary holds as victim, looking at the way in which Bloch has chosen to represent his victim and the way in which this differs from traditional Gothic victimology

Interestingly in this particular text, the process of being a victim and then becoming a heroine once the danger has been overcome is not so readily identifiable. Traditionally, Gothic heroines assume their status as a result of enduring and prevailing against the evil that has befallen them and when they manage to overcome these odds and succeed to outsmart or outrun the force of the active aggressor in the text, they are then granted the status of enduring heroine.

If we think back to *Otranto*'s Isabella or *The Italian*'s Ellena we can see evidence of the ways in which virtue is championed and courage rewarded in traditional Gothic writing. But what we find in Bloch's *Psycho* is an altogether different representation of female strength and heroism, for despite the fact that it is Mary who is the original victim, falling prey to Mother Bates' rage, it is not she who emerges successfully and heroically from the text, and instead that role is given to her sister, Lila.

At this point it is worth reminding ourselves that Mary whilst being hunted down by Mother Bates is also being chased down by the Private Investigator hired by her employer to find her and recover the stolen money. That she should find herself pursued by two different sources is interesting, and it is even more interesting that it is the seemingly innocent crime of accepting Norman's invitation to the house for supper, rather than the obvious crime of stealing the forty thousand dollars, for which she must pay the price. Her murder prevents her from absolving herself morally by returning the money, as she professes that she will do, and it is her ultimate status as unresolved and seemingly unrepentant criminal that prevents her from achieving any level of heroic status within the text; here Bloch has certainly remained true to Gothic form in that evil will not prosper.

There is a stark difference between the way in which Mary and her sister Lila are treated by Bloch in the text, and this is largely due to the concepts of honesty and integrity that are inherent in the novel. Arguably Mary herself brings about her own downfall, beginning as she does the chain of events that lead her to the Bates Motel. It is of course, a harsh price to pay, but nevertheless one that she brings upon herself. Bloch's treatment of Lila, on the other hand is much more sensitively crafted, and she is ultimately is portrayed as the good angel as opposed to Mary's bad angel. We remain sympathetic to Lila as her anxiety over the welfare of her sister is revealed and she pushes both Loomis and Arbogast into a more active search for her missing sibling. We admire her courage and determination and her ultimate resolve to do what she considers right by her sister. She demonstrates bravery as she enters the Bates house, and all of these virtues are rewarded and she achieves the status of true heroine of the text as she narrowly manages to avoid becoming Mother's next victim by the speedy advent and swift thinking of the hero of the text, Sam Loomis.

Evidently within *Psycho* there are a number of features that are identifiable as being traditionally Gothic, but more significantly there is much that Bloch has manipulated. Of course, the more obvious elements of the Gothic are still very much intact: the house, the suspense induced by sinister weather, well-placed thunder claps, secrets, lies and the inevitable revelation of that which has been kept hidden, frightening male figures and triumphant heroines. What makes this particular text so significant, however, is not Bloch's ability to spin a good old Gothic yarn, but to do it with such increasing complexity (combined with elements of detective fiction) that the text begins to take on greater meaning that its early (or first phase) Gothic predecessors.

We can see how this increase in complexity manifests itself if we take a moment to explore the differing roles of the corpse in *Psycho* and *The Old English Baron* (the corpse in *Psycho* being that of Mother Bates not Mary Crane or Detective Arbogast). Horrific as those murders may be, in modern crime fiction such murder is commonplace, and thus carries no real shock value for the reader. It is the disinterment, subsequent manipulation of and co-habitation with Mother Bates' decomposed corpse that is the most interesting of all the deaths and also the one that bears greatest resemblance to the secreted corpse in *The Old English Baron*.

Abjection and the Role of the Corpse

One of the defining features of first phase Gothic is the gentle way in which the death (or murder as it usually is) is presented to the reader. Although we are told in general terms what has happened, the exact details and the gore of the crime are largely kept from us. As reader we are kept at a respectable distance from the horror that has taken place and as a result of this the way in which we respond to the event is compromised. It is this aspect of distance and removal from the focus of the crime itself that is one of the primary differences between this early first phase Gothic and subsequent, later texts. Modern crime fiction grants us often uncomfortable proximity to the corpse, and this greater emphasis on the corpse within the text can indeed be seen in *Psycho*.

For those of us who read the text without having seen the film and do not know that Mother Bates is nothing more than a corpse, alive only in Norman's mind, the revelation and the true enormity of Norman's mental instability is not revealed until almost at the end of the book. It is of course Lila who makes the shocking discovery that Norman has not only been physically living with his mother's remains, but also that he has been moving, interacting and maintaining a filial relationship with it, and when Lila does so, the reader is also expected to share the horror of that which she has discovered:

> She screamed when she saw the old woman lying there, the gaunt, gray-haired old woman whose brown, wrinkled face grinned up at her in an obscene greeting.[113]

73

The proximity to the corpse that the reader is granted is certainly a far cry from the modesty that surrounded first phase Gothic texts, and in permitting greater access to this aspect of the text, the author is placing greater demands upon the reader in terms of his/her emotional response to and processing of the text itself. When considering the differing and more explicit ways in which the reader is presented with the corpse in these later novels it is interesting to explore the ways in which Julia Kristeva's theories on abjection can be applied to the texts.

At its most basic, abjection can be defined as the way in which a human being responds with horror to a particular event/occurrence that he/she is confronted with. It is that which occurs when identity, system and order (as we recognise them) are disturbed and there is subsequent collapse of understanding and coherence in something that we have hereto understood. There are, according to Kristeva, many situations in which abjection might occur, but essentially it will be characterised by those situations which, for somebody, will induce feelings and emotions of horror as meaning and cohesion are lost as a result of that which they are confronted with. In this respect abjection is an entirely individual experience, and not at all universal in how, where, when or why it happens.

Kristeva's theories on abjection can certainly be applied to *Psycho*, particularly in relation to the presence of the corpse of Mother Bates, presenting us as it does with a veritable blurring of the boundary between life and death and therefore interrupting our understanding of the proper path between life and death. Abjection occurs for Lila upon finding the corpse for two reasons, firstly the horror that she experiences upon seeing the corpse itself, but also because as a result of this Lila's understanding of the natural transition between life and death is momentarily suspended as she witnesses that which is not supposed to be; that is the presence of a dead body in what effectively is a live environment, the domesticity of what is essentially someone's home. That abjection occurs reminds us, as the reader, of Lila's humanity. That she reacts so appropriately to the horror that she witnesses seal her place as the true heroine of the text; she is ultimately a good and proper person, who, despite having her bravery tested to the absolute limits, still manages to emerge with her integrity and decency intact.

If Lila's abject reaction to the corpse earmarks her as human, what then can be said of Norman's seeming reverence for it? Certainly he does not react with horror towards it, rather he appears to reject the abject in the sense that he is actively trying to pursue, reclaim and maintain a 'relationship' with Mother through interaction with her corpse (the same can be said for the lack of horror demonstrated by the demonic Mr Hyde in Stevenson's work as *he* shows no remorse or horror towards the mangled body of the victim he has battered to death). Therefore we must conclude that Norman Bates (and Hyde too), if humanity is demonstrated by the ability to be abject, is not human, at least not by conventional standards. It is an interesting feature of the text, and represents another way in which Bloch has made significant movements forward from traditional Gothic, which simply did not permit us close enough access to the corpse for abjection to occur. Socially it is also a pertinent distinction to make – that our decency as human beings can be measured by the extent to which we are repulsed by the presence of the corpse within the text.

Of course Norman's relationship with the corpse is more than simply a means by which the author can demonstrate Norman's lack of normal human emotional responses. It is all to do with the theme of preservation that operates on a number of different levels within the story and all of which link in some way back to the desire inherent in the earliest Gothic fiction to survive and to procreate to ensure lineage at all costs. Superficially at least Norman harbours the corpse as a means of maintaining close physical proximity to Mother, and on the one hand one could interpret this need to be close to Mother and to nurture and care for her as best he can given the circumstances as a means of appeasing his guilt and atoning for the crime that he has committed. In all probability this is one logical explanation for the presence of the corpse, but it is because the presence of the corpse is so essential to Norman's ability to *survive* that the novel becomes inherently Gothic.

I am not suggesting for a minute that Norman wishes to procreate with his Mother, more that it is the theme of *survival* that has been taken from the traditional Gothic and manipulated into an environment where survival on a day to day basis becomes paramount to Norman, and the only way he can do this is to have Mother close to hand. Whereas early Gothic works were largely concerned with making provisions for and ensuring the family line for the future, *Psycho* is only concerned with the immediate present; the here and now of successful existence for Norman.

A New Direction for the Genre: Some Historical Context

As with all writing, however, it is interesting to consider whether a new direction within a text, such as the one here that Bloch appears to be making, is merely something that has been stumbled upon inadvertently or whether it is a deliberately crafted move. Certainly when considering the cultural context in which *Psycho* was written (1959), there are some clues. We already know that the ability to incorporate social and political observation into the story is something that is very typical of early Gothic, particularly many of those texts produced in the Gothic boom of the 1790s, and it would appear that in this respect, *Psycho* is no exception. Indeed, if we are to seriously consider the role of the French Revolution upon Gothic writing of the 1790s, then we absolutely must take into account the effect of the Korean War, the ongoing Cold War and America's involvement in the Vietnam War on Gothic writing of the late 50s and beyond.

In the late 1950s (and beyond) America was both a fragile and volatile place, and the cultural, social and political uncertainty of the period has been well documented:

> American society fractured more completely than it had at any time since
> the Civil War era. That fracturing seemed almost infinitely compound,
> as society broke along generational, racial, class, ethnic, regional,
> ideological, aesthetic and gender lines. Upheaval of one kind or another
> touched almost every aspect of private and public life. As public debate
> devolved into anger, confrontation and recrimination, civility was lost.[114]

The period has been described as being 'so tumultuous, intrusive and overwhelming that each person had to decide at some level... [to adopt] a new consciousness'[115], and there is sufficient historical documentation to support this. Since the late 1940s American political and social unease had been steadily growing. Communist theory and Red Scare had been spun and manipulated to such an extent by American Congress that it leeched into everyday life, personified into a terrible monster that threatened the upheaval of stable American domesticity. The culture was increasingly one of deep rooted paranoia and universal suspicion that itself threatened disintegration and fragmentation of society.

In recognising and understanding this then, is there suitable scope with which to interpret *Psycho*, and indeed at great many other modern crime novels as fitting metaphors for the societies in which they were created? It would appear that there is evidence to suggest that this is the case and that fictions that feature criminals and monsters 'answer the human need to personify free-floating fears, aggravated by the perplexing indeterminacy of the postmodern world.'[116]

If we assume this to be true, then we need to look at the exact ways and the extent to which Norman Bates has come to personify these 'free-floating fears', whilst attempting to define the exact nature of the fears themselves. It is interesting that it is through the detective aspect of the text rather than through the Gothic influence within the story that the degree of cultural anxiety and context are revealed. In traditional Gothic writing cultural unease is often revealed through ill-disguised metaphor and over–the-top melodrama (think of wildly aggressive tyrants governed by the demonic laws of patriarchal society and the threat they pose to the humble and innocent that stand in their way). In modern crime fiction the subtext is much more subtle. As readers we are limited to following the progress of the detective, and subsequently we are drip fed snippets of information that superficially at least relate to the crime but serve also to offer commentary upon and insight to the cultural anxieties of the time.

Given that *Psycho* was first published in 1959, if we are to explore this concept further we must therefore focus our attentions upon what 1950s American civilians were afraid of. Almost two decades of Communist-themed spin and propaganda had almost certainly affected the ways in which American citizens behaved towards each other and the levels of trust and esteem with which they regarded their fellow citizens. Above all the emphasis was on true Americanism and embracing all that which represented wholesome American life. Anything deemed 'un-American' in nature was regarded as deeply suspicious, and under Joseph McCarthy, the House Committee on Un-American Activities (created in 1938) became a veritable hot bed for rooting out those citizens within the United States deemed to be a threat to national security.

As they first appear to us in the text Norman Bates and his motel should pose as a relatively safe haven. Aside from his peculiar oddities, in the first instance Bates is represented as a mild-mannered, somewhat withdrawn, hard-working essentially decent man making a living whilst managing to care for his elderly mother. He is absolutely not a figure that we should be frightened of. He is in no way connectable to the concept of barbarianism, domination, terror and destruction that has come to epitomise and to represent the Communist threat as illustrated and documented in so much of the propaganda of the time.

It is this aspect of the hidden sinister that separates *Psycho* from so many of its contemporaries. Our instinct tells us not to fear Norman Bates, but evidently we must. He is on the one hand a nobody, insignificant and seemingly forgettable, yet paradoxically he is an everyman with unspeakably awful potential that is realised only through what appears to be the most innocuous of events, and this is altogether a much more frightening concept than confrontation with instantly recognisable tyranny. Norman Bates, if nothing else, reminds us just how careful we must be in choosing whom we trust and absolutely reiterates the message of early and French revolution era Gothic writing – that appearances can be so very deceptive. Bates is, perhaps, a fitting reminder as to where the real threat lies; not in imagination or perceived threats, but in the very real damage that we do to ourselves and to society as a whole by perpetuating these threats.

The novel explores the concept of the monster that lurks in our own back yard, rather than imagined danger that we believe we might be confronted with on a day to day basis. It uses elements of the Gothic coupled with a strong detective theme to explore this. Bates, complete with his seeming gentility and inoffensiveness, represents exactly that which has been allowed to grow quietly whilst the nation's back was turned, its attention elsewhere. He is not only a product of his own time and environment, but also that which poses the most danger to it.

Unlike early Gothic fiction whose narratives are largely driven by a demented, but somewhat understandable desire to survive and to procreate, *Psycho* carries with it a greater degree of sub-text and cultural unease than these earlier novels. Arguably a text that is deeply representative of the period in which it was written it demonstrates perfectly the joining of Gothic and detective fiction to produce a new fictional genre that is worthy of serious critical analysis.

CHAPTER FOUR

Internal Conflict and Red Menace: Evolution and Identity in Thomas Harris' *Red Dragon, The Silence of the Lambs, Hannibal* and *Hannibal Rising*

I F we are to accept Bloch's text as an early example of modern crime fiction whereby the Gothic and detective fiction become fused and that cultural anxieties and unease are reflected in the sub-text of the novel, then we would do well to look at an example of later modern crime fiction to understand to what extent the cultural context has shifted and the extent to which this shift manifests itself within the genre. One such example that fits the bill nicely is the series of Hannibal Lecter books written by Thomas Harris beginning in the early 1980s, widely credited with creating 'the current formula for mainstream serial killer fiction'[117] and of being 'indebted'[118] to the Gothic genre.

Across his texts Harris demonstrates not only heavy *Gothic* influence, but also a strong *detective* core, and it is the way in which he combines these two genres (essentially pitting the melodrama of the traditional Gothic against the attempted reason and logic of the traditional detective genre) that reveals most about the political and social unease of the time. In terms of the Gothic aspects of the texts, it is within *these* that the boldest statements about issues of identity and evolution are made, and it is understanding the way in which these two concepts are explored that will form the main topic for this chapter.

Because so much has already been done by other studies and critiques into the way in which Harris uses the Gothic genre, the focus of this chapter will be less *what* Harris does with the Gothic, and more so *why* he does what he does. The chapter will focus on the novels' social and political contexts specifically suggesting that the texts are absolutely representative of the tumultuous fallout of the turbulence that America experienced in the 1960s and 1970s.

In the previous chapter some commentary was made upon the social and political difficulties faced by America in the early years of the Cold War, and when it comes to interpreting the early Harris texts it needs to be remembered that not only would this upheaval have affected society at the time, but its repercussions would have been felt for many generations to come. It is *this* situation that Harris' novels are born from. Dolarhyde and Gumb, Graham and Starling are in effect products of 1960s America, children of instability and paranoia and to study them without making reference to this would be to ignore a large part of the novels' subtexts. In order to understand them in adulthood (as we find them in the texts) we need to fully understand their childhood and to do this effectively the text must expose the cultural anxieties of that time.

Simultaneous Hero/Villains and Villain/Victims: A New Level of Complexity

Of Harris' two earliest texts (*Red Dragon* 1981 *and The Silence of the Lambs* 1988*)*, it is *Red Dragon* that is the more traditionally Gothic. In the novel Dolarhyde takes on the role of the villain, Graham the hero (a deeply flawed version of the traditional hero, as we shall see in due course), the butchered families as the victims and Molly Graham the heroine. True to traditional Gothic form the villain in this particular text (Dolarhyde) demonstrates a simultaneous loathing of and a conflicting need for the women he obliterates as part of the process that he defines as his 'Becoming'[119].

Like Manfred before him, Dolarhyde has a distinct purpose (no matter how abhorrent that purpose might seem to everyone else) behind the crime he commits, and this purpose is linked to his own need to establish identity and future for himself through evolving from what he perceives to be his insignificant human form into the powerful Great Red Dragon. Just as Manfred became a victim of a society that clamoured for a male heir to continue patriarchal lineage in a feudal system, thus ensuring the longevity of the family's identity and status, Dolarhyde is also a victim of sorts too in needing to forge an identity for himself in a society that he understands as having for the most part ignored, shunned and mocked him for his entire life.

Red Dragon's Dolarhyde is an interesting character. Although unques-tionably villainous, Harris has carefully constructed a detailed personal history for him (in much the same way that Bloch detailed certain aspects of Bates' childhood) so that at certain parts of the text he is able to evoke pity for Dolarhyde and portray him as both villain *and* victim. It is this duality that makes Dolarhyde a much more compelling and complex char-acter than he would otherwise be. In providing insight into the two halves of personality in this way Harris is doing two important things with regard to our reading of the text. Firstly he is re-engaging with the nature-nurture debate that formed the basis for much 19th-century Gothic, and secondly he is re-visiting the recurring theme of the Gothic that ordered establishments and supposed places of safety often prove to be more dangerous than one would have thought possible. Certainly this is true of the ill-treatment that Dolarhyde receives at the hands of those who should protect him at both the orphanage and Grandmother's house. There is also much that is reminiscent of Victorian Gothic within the text, and this relates to the way in which Harris has given rise to Freudian theory of the return of the repressed. In detailing significant aspects of childhood it can be revealed to us exactly what is going on beneath the surface of the characters that we meet.

Certainly the concept of duality of character or of a split in human persona is strongly hinted at by the presence of quotes from Blake's *Songs of Innocence* and *Songs of Experience* that form a prologue of sorts to the text. Interestingly when we compare Dolarhyde with *Silence's* Gumb (who is given no such background to account for the conflict in *his* person-ality), Gumb becomes far less of a sustainable character and he, who should form such a strong part of the main plot, pales into insignificance alongside the development of the characters of Hannibal Lecter and Clarice Starling.

There is interesting duality too, in the construction of *Red Dragon's* almost-but-not-quite hero, Will Graham. Coerced out of retirement by Jack Crawford at the beginning of the book, Graham occupies a confusing role within the text. On the one hand he is ultimately responsible for the identi-fication of Dolarhyde (hero in this respect), but he is also deeply flawed and this is something new that Harris brings to the concept of traditional Gothic hero. Guilty of the murder of Garrett Hobbs and having spent time in a mental institute some years ago, the 'darker' side to Graham is clearly revealed when Lecter states that he and Will are 'just alike'[120]. It is with this statement that we as reader can fully understand the meaning behind Harris' use of Alphonse Bertillon's quote at the start of the book:

One can only see what one observes, and one observes only the things which are already in the mind [121]

Graham has 'a lot of trouble with taste'[122], picks apart conversation, looking for fault where none was intended, drinks too much and has the potential for emotional distance. Nevertheless he is the hero of the text because it is 'his bad luck to be the best'[123] and it is interesting Harris has given Graham to America as the one who will save them from Dolarhyde. Indeed it could be argued that in a society that is responsible for creating Dolarhyde then perhaps Graham, complete with flaws, is nothing more than we deserve.

Interestingly Graham's role as hero is not cemented within the text as at the end it is not he who finally kills Dolarhyde, and instead the slaying of the dragon is carried out by Molly, Graham's wife. That in the end it is she who not only manages to escape him, but manages to destroy him denotes a significant shift in the balance of power between male and female within this new breed of modern crime fiction. In allowing Molly to kill Dolarhyde, Harris is offering an alternative to the rather limiting (if not misogynistic) role that the heroine occupies in traditional Gothic writing. As if to empower her further, Harris allows her to make the decision at the end of the novel to take Willy back to her parents in Oregon and to walk out on her relationship with Graham. If all this seems a little harsh, then that is because it is; there simply is no room for sentimentalism or romantic whimsy in Harris' text.

Throughout the novel the picture that Harris paints of American society is troubling. Already we have ascertained that Graham, complete with faults is the best that the FBI can offer. Of course Graham is not even a federal agent and never has been; instead he is a last resort, someone who is drafted in when it becomes apparent that the FBI is no match for Dolarhyde. That national security is so reliant upon a misfit to find the answers for them is alarming if nothing else. We will see the extent to which this lack of confidence in the FBI and its protocol manifests itself and becomes a recurrent theme within modern crime fiction when we look to the construction of Cornwell's *The Last Precinct* in Chapter 6 of this text.

Evidently the Harris texts are far from 'unqualified celebrations of the modern law enforcement wizardry of the state or its status as protector of middle-class civilisation'[124] and Graham (like Starling) consequently operates as an outsider whom the FBI desperately need to succeed where they themselves have failed. That Dolarhyde remains so elusive for the most part of the novel is perhaps more indicative of Harris' continuation of the early

Gothic trend for the villain to become a physical manifestation of whatever is threatening society at the time of writing. In keeping Dolarhyde at large Harris is hinting at problems of a much larger scale than simply the desired apprehension of one deranged man. Of course Dolarhyde at the physical level is a dangerous being. That he butchers (seemingly at random) entire families in one swoop is frightening, but he is much more than this too, representing as he does the complete invasion and destabilising of successful suburban America. Whilst he remains at large American civilians are under the belief that there is a traitor in their midst; one that threatens to destroy everything they have worked so hard to achieve. Whilst uncaught he is faceless and unidentifiable, and his potential to undermine society is without limit.

So what great 'fear' does Dolarhyde represent? Certainly it is impossible pick apart his greater significance and threat without understanding the cultural anxiety that he was born into, and this anxiety is specifically America's great fear and paranoia regarding Communism during the Cold War. Certainly there is the suggestion that the persona of the 'Red Dragon' that Dolarhyde adopts for himself originates from the Blake painting that he is so taken with, but the 'Red' could very well also be interpreted as having Communist connotations. There is evidence to suggest that the feelings of paranoia experienced by American society as they seek to protect themselves from the Dragon is akin to the threat from Communism that characterised so much of the 1950s, 60s and even the 70s. Red Scare – whether real or perceived – shaped an entire nation's thinking and outlook as the core stability of American society was undermined and the illusion of faceless Communists stalking the streets generated huge levels of suspicion amongst American nationals.

In a country 'preoccupied with the Communist menace'[125] American children during the 1950s were expected to 'respect authority, work hard in school, fear Communism and love God and country'[126] and within *Red Dragon* this preoccupation seems to have come at the expense of paying sufficient attention to other issues affecting domestic harmony. This state of affairs is crucial to our understanding of not only where Dolarhyde came from, but also exactly what he is and what he represents. In giving us such detailed information about the abuse and neglect suffered by the child Dolarhyde at Brother Buddy's orphanage, Grandmother's house and also at the hands of the Vogt children, Harris could indeed be suggesting that in devoting so much energy into the *perceived* threat of Communism that the *actuality* and *reality* of what was amiss in society at that time was ignored. In this case Dolarhyde becomes the result of this neglect and the revenge that he takes upon that part of society that failed him is exacting; whilst the nation's back was turned no-one noticed the monster growing in its own back yard.

In Harris' second Lecter novel *The Silence of the Lambs*, Harris essentially sticks to a similar formula with regards to his main plot and that is the hunt for the serial killer Jame Gumb who has been abducting women, killing them and taking sections of their skin. The hunt for the killer is also managed outside of conventional FBI governance and in this case rests largely in the hands of trainee Clarice Starling. There are, however, a number of significant alterations and changes that Harris has made to the successful *Red Dragon* format, the most significant of these being the multiple plots at work within the text and the manner in which they run alongside the main plot, detracting attention away from that which *should* take centre stage, that is the murders of the women.

This is perhaps most evident in the way in which Harris handles the development of Jame Gumb, the character who *should* occupy the role of villain in the text and consequently become one of the (if not *the* most) important characters. The difference between the amounts of information that we are given about him compared to the amount that was detailed about Dolarhyde is startling. Throughout the text he remains an enigma and is definable only through the horrendous acts he has committed. Whilst it is true that we can glean *some* information about Gumb's mother and his childhood from the text, the information that we are presented with is nowhere near as explicit as it was for Dolarhyde. The result of this is of course, as was mentioned earlier in this chapter, that Gumb becomes hugely overshadowed by the character of the alluring and mysterious Dr Lecter.

The Move into Evolution

Despite this variation in the degree of information revealed about the killer, there are clear parallels between the villains Dolarhyde and Gumb, as both perceive themselves to be involved in a process of change that will bring about a stronger and more absolute sense of identity for them. They are both evolving characters trying to move from a state of instability (with the very strong suggestion that these instabilities are a direct consequence of neglect – by the state and by the parent – in childhood) into a more stable existence. It is this concept of evolution (rather than the devolution that defined Bates) that most clearly demonstrates the greatest change that Harris brings to the direction of this latest wave of modern crime fiction.

In the case of Francis Dolarhyde his 'Becoming'[127] is part of his search for identity and recognition by achieving power and control. He has seized upon the masculine dominance and virility shown in the Blake painting *The Great Red Dragon and the Woman Clothed with the Sun* and for him the Dragon of the painting represents all that he is not and all that he wishes to be and to have. The image of the woman helpless below the Dragon as it waits to devour the child has found a willing host in Dolarhyde who interprets its meaning to suit his own twisted definition of strength and success.

For Gumb the process of evolution and change is a more *physical* process, as he seeks to create for himself a suit of woman's skin made from real harvested hide. Gumb's journey of metamorphosis is symbolised by the presence of the moths, whose pupae are inserted deep into the throat of his victims. But he, like Dolarhyde, views his crimes less as actual crimes and more the taking of what is rightfully his in order that he may begin to thrive. In Gumb's eyes his victims cease to be women and become little more than carriers of the female skin that he so desires; he values them only for what they will provide him and never refers to them as anything other than 'it':

> 'Wash yourself. Take it off and wash yourself all over, or you'll get the hose.' And an aside to the dog as the voice faded, 'Yes it will get the hose, wont' it, Darlingheart, yes it *will!*'[128]

Dolarhyde similarly dehumanises his victims as he regards them as having purpose only in relation to his own process of change:

> Dolarhyde felt that Lecter knew the unreality of the people who die to help you in these things – understood that they are not flesh, but light and air and color and quick sounds quickly ended when you change them. Like balloons of color bursting. That they are more important for the changing, more important than the lives they scrabble after, pleading.[129]

The fact that both characters are seeking to change and to develop, to evolve into altogether different physical beings, does indeed demonstrate a significant change to the genre. Whereas Bates was content to sit back and to manage and enjoy his relationship with Mother by himself (a co-existence and harmony that was only shattered by the arrival of Mary Crane), Dolarhyde and Gumb are the complete opposite. That both of these characters are so *actively* looking for the means by which they can alter themselves, to evolve and to change, signifies a much greater degree of choice and depicts a degree of acute deliberation that was absent from Bloch's text. Unhappy with their lots they seek that which they feel will make them complete and what this shows us, rather terrifyingly, is what a danger ambition becomes when it is placed into the wrong hands. In actively deciding not just to sit at home, thus rendering themselves impotent and incapacitated, both Dolarhyde and Gumb, in attempting to realise their ambition and assert themselves, move from the realms of reactive murderer (the role that Bates holds) and into the domain of active predator.

At the time at which Harris was writing, American post-Cold-War society was keen to re-acquaint itself with the concepts of identity, assertiveness and power, and eager to rediscover the quality of existence as typified by the values and rights of the American Dream as it was defined in James Truslow Adams' 1931 book *The Epic of America*. Indeed Adams' sentiments of opportunity and equality, and of existence where each man should be able to realise his full potential is very much what *Red Dragon* and *The Silence of the Lambs* are all about. Both novels offer a fascinating and twisted understanding of the statement from America's Declaration of Independence (1776) that 'all men are created equal, that they are endowed by their Creator with certain unalienable Rights, that among these are Life, Liberty and the pursuit of Happiness'[130]. Certainly the concepts and the themes of the Declaration have a very strong resonance within these two Thomas Harris texts; not only are Dolarhyde and Gumb acting only in pursuit of their happiness, by all accounts they have been taught by society that to pursue happiness is not only their God-given right, it is what is expected of them.

Clarice Starling: 'The Honey in the Lion'[131]

Given the similarities and significance in what both Dolarhyde and Gumb are trying to achieve, it is unusual that Gumb himself occupies such a small role within *The Silence of the Lambs*. Despite holding the role of active villain and despite the tendency for the active villain to be the most compelling and interesting character in traditional Gothic writing, Harris inverts this theme and instead Gumb's presence within the novel is greatly overshadowed by Harris' re-introduction of the character of Dr Lecter and the introduction of FBI trainee, Clarice Starling. Harris' careful manipulation of the Gothic form allows for Starling and Lecter, rather than Gumb, to take centre stage and resultingly the novel becomes less about the actual crimes that have been committed by Gumb and more about the journey of self-discovery and consolidation of identity for Clarice Starling as Harris gives to her the same level of personal history that he did to Dolarhyde in *Red Dragon*.

The development of relationship between Starling and Lecter not only serves to set the stage for the follow-up text *Hannibal* but also offers a heavily Gothic-influenced romanticism that is almost fairy-tale like in its beauty and the beast connotations. As a 'romance' it is far more developed and complex than romantic relationship that existed between Dolarhyde and Reba McClane, and on closer inspection is can indeed be seen that the role that Reba holds in *Red Dragon* is not very different from the role held by Mary Crane in *Psycho*. Rather than offering genuine romantic interest for Dolarhyde, Reba instead serves to become the link between Dolarhyde's *public* persona (the position that he holds at Gateway Film Laboratory) and his *private* space (that is the way in which he conducts himself in Grandmother's house).

Dolarhyde, like Bates, continues to live under the oppressive shadow of a powerful and dominant matriarchal figure, but whereas Bates' behaviour and devolution was very much representative of his feelings of guilt and love for Mother, Dolarhyde's attempts at evolution are very much indicative of his need to break away from Grandmother's influence and construct an independent existence for himself. The change that he desires for himself is pitched alongside the power that Dolarhyde perceives to be emitting from the Blake painting *The Great Red Dragon and the Woman Clothed with the Sun* and, certainly until the introduction of Reba into the text and into Dolarhyde's life, it is a power that he seems to be in control of. Reba, in acting as a physical and emotional link between the public and the private halves of Dolarhyde's life forces a meeting betwixt the two and the result is that he begins to lose control of himself as the Dragon seizes power (just as Mother began to do in *Psycho*) and Dolarhyde loses his final grasp on 'reality', descending even deeper into madness.

If we accept Mary Crane and Reba as both being catalysts that either set off a sequence of events, or significantly alter those that are already occurring, then we must also look at the way in which Clarice Starling is able to manipulate the minds of those around her and the way in which she too manages to influence the direction of the narrative. Indeed the role that Starling occupies within the text is very interesting. From gutsy rookie she fast becomes the hero of the hour as she manages to save Catherine Baker Martin from Jame Gumb. Her success is short lived however, and by the opening of *Hannibal* we find her downtrodden and relentlessly victimised by the vindictive Paul Krendler, by the end of this novel her position has changed again and she now occupies the role of Lecter's lover.

In terms of her position that she holds within *The Silence of the Lambs* and the significant proportion of the text that Harris has allotted to her, it is reasonable to consider the novel as less interested in the dynamics of the crimes that have been committed and more concerned with the intellectual and emotional makeup of those responsible for solving them. Certainly this aspect of increased interest in the investigators of crimes rather than the criminals is something we will look at in greater detail when we come to examine the novels of Ian Rankin and Patricia Cornwell.

But for now how do we explain the dramatic fall from grace that affects Starling across the two novels *The Silence of the Lambs* and *Hannibal*? Without doubt her role in both texts is complicated. Chosen by Crawford to interview Lecter in an attempt to surreptitiously gain information that might assist in the hunt for Buffalo Bill he admits to her he has enquired after her progress in the Academy, confessing to her that he 'didn't pick [her] out of a hat' and that whilst at UVA she had asked him a 'couple of interesting questions'[132]. In terms of the qualities that she displays that grab Lecter's attention she presents herself as honest, perseverant and in possession of a good deal of integrity. She demonstrates an appropriate degree of humility during her 'sessions' with Lecter and shows that she is neither a fool nor one who suffers fools and foolishness gladly. Unruffled by Lecter's incredulity that Crawford would send a *'trainee* to interview'[133] him she responds with grit:

> 'I'm still at the Academy, yes,' Starling said, 'but we're not discussing the FBI – we're talking psychology. Can you decide for yourself if I'm qualified in what we talk about?'[134]

That she admits openly to being a trainee rather than shying away from her inexperience demonstrates an inner core of strength that Lecter responds to. Unlike Chilton who will willingly allow people to assume that his 'Dr' status refers to a medical degree rather than to the PhD that he holds, Starling is refreshingly honest and open. Ultimately it is the fact that Starling is so *eye-catching* that she holds such a pivotal role in this text and also *Hannibal*. Not only does she catch Lecter's eye for the reasons outline above, she also caught Crawford's professional eye (it was this that essentially brought her to Lecter's cell). She catches also, rather regretfully, the eye of Paul Krendler which is an attraction that will prove over time to be so detrimental to her career.

Her success in *Silence of the Lambs* is largely due to the way in which she triumphs against each of these 'interests'. She will not compromise herself with Paul Krendler, rises above the role of pawn and plaything that Crawford originally cast for her and manages to draw sufficient information from Lecter and to see through his bluff in time to save Catherine Baker Martin. She is worthy, without doubt, of the title of 'warrior' that Lecter gives her in *Hannibal*:

> You are a warrior, Clarice. The enemy is dead, the baby safe. You are a warrior. The most stable elements, Clarice, appear in the periodic table, roughly between iron and silver. Between iron and silver. I think that is appropriate for you.[135]

The difficulties that Starling experiences as lone female in a masculine world are very much evident at the scene of the Potter Funeral Home where she has been called to carry out the initial assessment of the body of Kimberly Emberg. Sexually appraised by the deputies on her way into the Home she is then very much relegated to the sidelines by Crawford as he states that 'this kind of sex crime has some aspects that I'd rather say...just between us men...'[136] Not one to shy away from honesty she later tells Crawford that his apparent shunning of her was wrong; 'Starling couldn't let it go. "It matters, Mr Crawford."'[137] That she possesses all the attributes necessary to succeed in such a masculine environment is arguably one of the reasons why she is successful in her identification of Gumb and rescuing of Catherine Baker Martin. She demonstrates guts and determination and through attributing these characteristics to her Harris rejects the stereotype of marginalised female that was such a recurring character in early Gothic writing. Rather he empowers her that she may be able to significantly shape and to a certain extent control the way in which the narrative unfolds. In this respect the role that Starling holds within *Silence* is not so very different from the influential role held by Mina Harker in Stoker's *Dracula*. Similarly both women are credited with possessing minds and brains that are recognised as being not only useful, but essential in resolving the problems that surround them. The advancement within the genres (both the Gothic and in modern crime fiction) is of course that this recognition comes from the men within the texts, who are neither stupid nor narrow minded enough to ignore the reality of the assets that both Mina and Starling bring to the mix.

Careful not to overstep the mark, however, Harris is clever in the way in which he manages to retain and hold on to enough of her femininity that we as reader do not feel alienated by her and fail to respond to her plight. He does this through the details of her upbringing that are revealed to us through her discussions with Dr Lecter. Once Starling's grief surrounding the death of her father and her humanity with regard to her desire to save the horse Hannah is exposed, her identity is sufficiently constructed to permit us to sympathise with and to understand her.

In keeping with traditional Gothic motif there are trace elements of the theme of beauty and the beast in the developing relationship between Starling and Lecter. However, whereas in early Gothic works this theme is largely defined by the pursuit of the beauty by the beast for sexual motivation, Lecter's pursuit of Starling is intellectual and probing in the way it is constructed. If we are correct in our understanding of the novel as primarily to do with issues of identity and the way in which confusion regarding identity can manifest itself in the behaviour of those who struggle to find one for themselves, then we must recognise Starling's interactions with the *psychiatrist* Dr Lecter rather than the *monster* Dr Lecter as pivotal in the way in which her identity is not only revealed to us in the novel, but also that it is through these sessions that her identity is actually *constructed*.

Understanding the Sub-Plots: A Reflection on Social Anxiety

Earlier in this chapter reference was made to the way in which the aftermath of the Cold War and anti-Communist propaganda was still very much being felt in 1980s America. Dolarhyde, Gumb, Graham and Starling were labelled as being children of 1960s America, with the suggestion that this insecure background would materialise somehow in the adult attitudes and behaviours of each. Regardless of the occupations that they each hold within the texts, be they criminal or a Federal Agent, what each of these characters share is a fundamental lack of understanding of who or what they are. Issues surrounding their identities arise from each of them being heavily influenced by some event or events in their past that have not been truly resolved and resultingly their identities, specifically their places in the world, are compromised. In understanding the ways in which issues of trust and stability in American society began to break down in the years following the beginning of the Cold War then certainly the issues affecting each of the characters identified above should be easier to understand.

For the purposes of clarity it should be pointed out that although there are many differing opinions as to when the Cold War actually began, I am defining it as a direct consequence of the matters arising during the Yalta Conference of 1945 and ending with the dissolution of the Soviet Union in

1991. During this period US intelligence and military initiatives were almost exclusively focused on raising awareness of and eradicating the Communist threat. Perhaps the most significant of these initiatives was the establishment of the American CIA in 1947. Issues of national security were by this time a major concern for the American Government and had been in the years even pre-dating the Second World War. Between 1934 and 1937 a Special Committee was set up to investigate propaganda, specifically Nazi propaganda that threatened to undermine American Society. In 1937 this Committee was replaced by the House Committee on Un-American Activities whose focus was to investigate subversive and treacherous activity on a more general scale, but with explicit reference to Communist activity within the United States. As suspicion grew and paranoia increased American society became saturated with anti-Communist propaganda which reached its height in the 1950s as the Committee issued and distributed leaflets, booklets and propaganda films detailing the Communist threat into schools, workplaces and into the general media. Certainly American preoccupation with the Communist menace was largely responsible for American involvement in the Korean War, the Bay of Pigs Invasion, the Cuban Missile Crisis, the Vietnam War and the invasion of Grenada.

Although each of these events significantly affected American society and American faith in its military and governing bodies, the most significant of these is of course the Vietnam War, and the extent to which this catastrophic American failure and embarrassment manifests itself within the texts simply cannot be ignored.

Quite simply Vietnam was a war that the Americans believed they would win. Unquestioned faith in US military weaponry, tactics and strategy simply did not anticipate that the outcome would be anything other American victory. Simple in theory, but in practice a different story altogether. American involvement in the war, and ultimately that war itself, ended in 1975 when the capital city of South Vietnam, Saigon, was captured and subsequently surrendered to the North and the two sides were unified under Communist control. The effect on America following the failure to retain Saigon and defeat the Communist North was immense. They had underestimated the strength and determination of their opponents. Never before had a war been given such media attention and images of the evacuation of the American military from Saigon and the surrounding areas were relayed around the world. American society learnt some harsh lessons about infallibility and cultural identity following a war that was not only costly in terms of financial loss, but also in terms of the immense loss of life (both military and civilian) experienced by themselves, both Vietnamese sides,

Cambodia and Laos.

The implications of this loss are clear to see in Harris' first text, *Red Dragon*. As outlined earlier in this chapter the novel concentrates upon the failure of the American FBI to contain and apprehend (at least until the intervention of Will Graham) the destructive force of the Red Dragon. Given the political context of the novel itself it would be a mistake to under-estimate the Communist connotations and metaphorical significance that is evident within the very title of the text.

The text has much to say about the role and responsibility of the American media in exploiting and manipulating fear, of the inappropriate-ness of uncontrolled media access and the intrusion into the private world of individuals by unscrupulous and manipulative individuals. When Freddy Lounds the journalist is introduced to us he is described as an 'obnoxious fellow'[138] caught trying to photograph the Leeds' bodies as they arrive at the Lombard Funeral Home. His insensitivity and inappropriateness is revealed as he asks 'How does this guy compare with Lecter? Does he do them – ?'[139] and Graham's disgust is equally explicit as he replies 'Lounds, you write lying shit and *The National Tattler* is an asswipe.'[140] The extent to which Lounds, as sole representative of the gutter press in the novel, will go to manipulate a story is also evident in the way in which he crops the photo-graph taken of Graham outside Chesapeake to read only 'Criminally Insane'. [141]

However, the true extent of the exploitative nature of this type of press is detailed in the manner in which the *Tattler's* attitude to cancer is explained:

> The *Tattler* could afford to pay him well because the paper found cancer
> very lucrative...the relatives of the dying...are desperate for anything
> hopeful. Marketing surveys showed that a bold 'New Cure for Cancer'
> or 'Cancer Miracle Drug' cover line boosted supermarket sales of any
> *Tattler* issue by 22.3 per cent...The standard story featured an optimistic
> five paragraphs in ten point, then a drop to eight point, then to six
> point before mentioning that the 'miracle drug' was unavailable...
> Freddy earned his money turning them out, and the stories sold a lot of
> *Tattlers*.[142]

Lounds of course pays the ultimate price for his lack of journalistic integrity. Seized by Dolarhyde he is asked by the 'Dragon' why he prints 'lies'[143] and in a message that could certainly be interpreted as Harris voicing a concern that press and reporters of this kind need to be contained and controlled, the Dragon bites off Lounds' lips and sets him on fire, ensuring, somewhat ironically, that Lounds will become his own cover story and that sales of the next issue of the *Tattler* will soar. That it falls to the Dragon to silence Lounds is also not without irony, as in the past it is something that Crawford himself has tried to do, but failed: 'I reamed him out, much good it did.'[144] Reigning in the press, it seems, is yet another area in which the FBI falls short.

The FBI is not the only institution to come under attack within the novel. There are also misgivings and reservations about the failure to offer safety and security to the young boy Dolarhyde at Brother Buddy's orphanage. There is also an unmistakable message that to assume comfort and solace from and within the arms of your own family is not only naive but downright dangerous as Francis is exposed to horrific abuse as the hands of Grandmother. The child effectively becomes a propaganda tool himself as he used to exploit the absolute meaningless of the word 'family' and all the connotations of love and togetherness that it promotes as Grandmother uses him to sabotage the Vogts' electoral campaign.

It appears that what Harris is doing, given the context of American government and military strategists' overwhelming failure to contain and to control the Communist menace, is to begin to subtly strip away and force us to question our belief in that which should give us comfort, and it is through the detective aspect to the text that he is able to do this. In much the same way that Bloch was able to expose cultural concerns and political unease through the movements of Arbogast, so too does Harris exploit wavering faith in institutional structures by having the FBI fail in apprehending Dolarhyde, Gumb and even Lecter once he has escaped. Whilst it is important that both Graham and Starling are supported by the FBI it is paramount to remember that neither one of them is actually an active agent within the Bureau. It is a small distinction surely, but one that is fundamental in evaluating and understanding the cultural significance of the texts.

Certainly this uncertainty and lack of faith surrounding the capabilities of the FBI is not lost on Hannibal Lecter in *The Silence of the Lambs* as he seeks to systematically expose every aspect of vulnerability that surrounds Clarice Starling and attempts to shatter her belief in the integrity and moral surety of the FBI. Brutally reminding her that she 'won't have this one either, once they're through using'[145] her and mocking her by suggesting to her that Crawford's interest in her may not be at all to do with her capabilities as an agent, he takes a great deal of pleasure in belittling and intimidating her and this is something that Starling recognises; '...he enjoys seeing the destruction of faith, it's his favourite thing.'[146] That she proves to him and to us as reader that she is more than capable of withstanding his attack is absolutely to her credit and, as mentioned earlier, one of the reasons she triumphs both professionally and personally at the end of the text.

The pleasure that Lecter takes in other people's misfortune, especially when that misfortune occurs whilst they are in the act of demonstrating their faith in supposed save havens, is again evident in the pleasure and glee that he derives from collecting information about church collapses. The irony that worshippers should suffer so profoundly at the hands of He who should protect them is nothing but a source of amusement for him as he states:

> I collect church collapses, recreationally. Did you see the recent one in Sicily? Marvellous. The façade fell on sixty-five grandmothers at a special Mass. Was that evil? If so, who did it? If He's up there, He just loves it, Officer Starling. Typhoid and swans – it all comes from the same place.[147]

The role that Lecter holds as destroyer of dreams across these two early texts is crucial to the way in which we are to understand the status of American faith and confidence in all things institutional at that particular period in time; essentially he is there simply to remind us of the folly of blind faith.

The systematic failing of the FBI is a theme that is also very much a part of *The Silence of the Lambs*, and the implication that the FBI alone is simply not up to the job is impossible to overlook. That in this example Crawford is dependent upon the combined efforts of a trainee and an incarcerated psychopath to hunt down Jame Gumb speaks volumes about American faith in its investigative forces and established institutions. Such a scathing attack upon the FBI as Harris seems to be making is born from its existence in a society that has lost its faith and its power to believe.

It is an aspect of the text, and indeed an aspect inherent in serial killer fiction that recurs with such frequency that to ignore it would be to miss an important part of the meaning of these texts. Within these early Harris novels the 'destabilisation of solid systems and symbols is the true agenda'[148], and frequent loss of 'moral surety'[149] is a recurrent theme. As a result of this deliberate attempt by authors to question and undermine our unwavering trust in 'solid systems' the detective plots of modern crime fiction texts often "operate within an ominously Gothic environment where the daily practice of morality and justice constantly slides away from idealistic centers, epitomizing a destabilising strategy common to Gothic fiction."[150] Certainly the *degree* to which institutional systems fail within the texts is significant, but what is equally important in light of this is the increased *need* for individuals to understand (and also to create or reinforce) their identities as a direct consequence of these catastrophic failings.

The Importance of Identity

Interestingly across these two texts and across the entire range of characters that we come across it is Lecter who seems to be the most at ease with who and what he is, having none of the issues of identity that seem to be such a part of Dolarhyde, Gumb, Graham and Starling. That he of all the characters should be so comfortable within his own skin is interesting, if not ironic, and it is something that we need to question. At its most basic level we could interpret Lecter's composure and understanding of himself as a reflection upon his nationality – specifically the fact that he is not an American. If we are to accept that the four characters already mentioned are a product of a deeply unsettled and insecure America, living examples of the social plight of American citizens then it would be logical to assume that Lecter, not being American, is unaffected by such issues of national anxiety. Put simply, he is not an American and therefore why should he bear any of the markings of or be at all troubled by the situation that Americans find themselves in following the Cold War and the aftermath of Vietnam?

Also perplexing (given the nature of the crimes that he has committed) is Lecter's chosen occupation of psychology. Without doubt there is a significant degree of conflict in the *capacity* to heal and to nurture that the profession requires and the *actuality* of the savagery and brutality that he displayed in the crimes that he committed. Perhaps if we are to accept that Will Graham, complete with flaws, is all that America deserves in the quest to save them from the Dragon, then one can also assume that Lecter, with his cannibalistic appetite is all that Americans (who are ultimately consumed by inward-looking suspicion and paranoia) deserve in their quest to heal themselves.

One thing that is definite, however, is that Lecter is not only comfortable with who he is, but that he is not about to create excuses in an attempt to create false justification for the crimes he has committed. When pressed by Starling into completing the questionnaire in order to discover 'what happened' to him"[151] that he ended up becoming a multiple murderer his response is brutally frank:

> Nothing happened to me, Officer Starling. I happened. You can't reduce
> me to a set of influences. You've given up good and evil for behaviourism,
> Officer Starling. You've got everybody in moral dignity pants – nothing
> is ever anybody's fault. Look at me, Officer Starling. Can you stand to
> say I'm evil? Am I evil, Officer Starling?[152]

Arguably it is Lecter's assertion that he is what he is simply because that
is what he has chosen to be is a great part of the allure of his character. That
he is so completely unquantifiable is unquestionably part of his 'charm' as a
character and it is interesting why, with this in mind, Harris in his next
novels *Hannibal* and *Hannibal Rising* chose to demystify the enigma and
divulge so much information about Lecter's childhood that it does indeed
become possible to provide comprehensive reasons and generate complete
understanding as to why Lecter came to commit the acts that he did.

Within *Hannibal* there are a number of ways in which Harris re-engages
with early Gothic form. The novel opens in Washington and as it does we
are re-introduced to Starling who, no longer one of the FBIs bright young
stars, instead occupies a position as a 'veteran'[153] of surveillance operations
whose career has been thwarted and sabotaged by somebody up at Buzzard's
Point who 'hates'[154] her. Unenthusiastic and demoralised, Starling's frustration is revealed to us as we learn that during the briefing before the Evelda
Drumgo take down that once she 'would have deferred to these men. Now
they didn't like what she was saying, and she had seen too much to care.'[155]

From the outset Harris' intention to set up Starling's role as Gothic
heroine is exposed. In the shoot-out she loses her friend and ally John
Brigham and is subsequently made scapegoat for the failed operation. It is at
her moment of deepest despair that Dr Lecter is brought into the text
through the letter that he writes to her which in turn exposes his role as
Gothic villain at this early stage in the novel. In a letter that exhibits as
much mockery as it does concern for Starling's plight, the complexity of the
relationship between her and Lecter is revealed. Effectively this letter
(combined with Crawford's liking and respect for her) saves her career, as in
a move that reaffirms *his* role as Starling's 'hero', Crawford is able to offer
her an alternative position in chasing up the lead to Lecter's whereabouts
that the letter has provided.

It would be naive however to assume that these characters stay within
these niche roles for the duration of the text, or that they are as simple to
define as this initial explanation might seem. This is of course not the case
at all, and in a style that echoes later Gothic convention, Harris' characters
are multi-layered and able to move around within the traditionally tight

limitations of character type. Lecter himself is not the only villain or monster within the text; there is arguable monstrosity in the way in which Krendler relentlessly victimises and bullies Starling, in the way in which Lecter himself is pursued by the warped Mason Verger and also the manner in which Rinaldo Pazzi is revealed to be fundamentally corrupt and will stop at nothing to get his financial reward. The role(s) of victim too are equally as cloudy. Certainly at the top of the list is Starling (at least at the beginning of the novel), but up there alongside her are the abused Margot Verger and even Lecter himself becomes victim once he is seized and exposed to torture at the hands of Mason's employees.

It is of course through the information that is revealed to us about Mischa, Lecter's sister, that the true extent of Lecter's role and capacity as victim is brought to light. As a consequence of this revelation the whole mystery that surrounds the enigmatic character of Dr Lecter is undone. In constructing a past just as detailed as was done for Francis Dolarhyde in *Red Dragon*, Harris is effectively forcing his readers to understand Lecter and the crimes that he has committed and demanding that we ask ourselves if, as a result of his upbringing and the trauma he suffered as a result of the death of his sister, that the real monster does not lie within Lecter himself. Should this be the case then the next question we are forced to address is where exactly does the monstrosity lie?

It is not until we read *Hannibal Rising* that the full extent of the horrors endured by the child Lecter are fully revealed. Having fled the family home to escape German troops advancing through Lithuania under Operation Barbarossa, the Lecter family seek shelter within the assumed safety of their hunting lodge and exist there quite happily until the entire group, with the exception of Hannibal and Mischa, are killed during an attack upon a Soviet tank by a Nazi military aircraft. Shortly after this the two children are found and captured by a group of wandering and starving military renegades who take Mischa from Hannibal and kill and cannibalise her.

In evaluating the Gothic features that are present across *Hannibal* and *Hannibal Rising* it becomes clear that rather than simply alluding to or suggesting that cultural context might have had some effect on the behaviour of the central character, Harris is absolutely explicit in the effect that he claims the Second World War had on Lecter's upbringing. Certainly within the context of Lecter's childhood we can at the very least begin to understand where his murderous intent and cannibalistic tendencies arise from. Does this excuse him from what he has done? Absolutely not, but nevertheless it does serve to answer some poignant questions.

Of course there is much debate, specifically to do with the critical reviews that each of these novels received as to whether the demystification of Hannibal Lecter is at all necessary in the first place, and there is strong argument to suggest that in exposing Lecter's upbringing Harris has perhaps inadvertently made him somewhat less alluring:

> This is what Thomas Harris' readers would least like to hear from Harris' flesh-eating celebrity, Dr. Hannibal Lecter. "I deeply regret any pain I might have caused for the victims and their families. For years I have helplessly battled the problem that caused me to misbehave. I intend to seek treatment for it immediately.[156]

Certainly there is a degree of truth when we consider that 'if a character such as Lecter is explained as himself a victim of some original trauma, he is no longer fascinating as an avatar of absolute evil. It was that fascination... that fuelled those novels'[157].

Arguably this is the case, and by exposing Lecter's unfortunate personal history Harris has, perhaps unintentionally caused Lecter to become far less of an appealing character than he had previously been. Paradoxically whilst our interest in Lecter wanes the more we learn about his history, the more interested we become in Starling as we are forced to evaluate the way in which *she* responds to *his* plight. From their initial relationship as trainee and 'mentor' that began in *The Silence of the Lambs*, throughout the course of *Hannibal* the level of dominancy and control between them is constantly changing and by the end of the novel they seem to have reached an equilibrium of power.

To this effect this novel is as much about evolution and change as were *Red Dragon* and *The Silence of the Lambs*. It is concerned with the issue to such an extent that when Lecter reveals to Starling his belief in the reversal of time and going backwards in an attempt to bring Mischa back to life, it is Starling herself who rejects this aspect of devolution in favour of a more evolutionary process asking Lecter rather than giving up *her* place in the world for Mischa, if there is not 'room' within him 'for Mischa'[158] Certainly it seems that across the four novels there is a great emphasis placed upon the need within each of the central characters to evolve in order to generate satisfactory identity for themselves. Obviously the context of this desire for identity is different within each of the novels and resultingly the path that each character opts for in order to evolve differs, but essentially across the texts the theme is the same.

As a consequence of this interest in evolution and identity, the detective aspect that is the hunt for the killer becomes almost secondary to the main plot, and instead merely serves to demonstrate the ineffectiveness of a structured institution to exert and maintain control over individuals who wish to operate outside of the boundaries of acceptable behaviour. This same failure was present in *Psycho*, and it was essentially down to Lila Crane rather than productive law enforcement operatives that Norman Bates was apprehended. In the Harris texts, just as in the Bloch text, the failure by the authorities to catch the criminals is one of the strongest metaphors for social context and demonstrates most effectively the sheer force of the rampant monster against the weakness and fallibility of mere man.

An Exclusively American Phenomenon?

That there are marked differences between the evolutionary and devolutionary processes between *Psycho* and each of the Harris texts is obvious, but what they *are* linked by is the ongoing issue of identity (or the ongoing issue of *lack* of identity to be specific). Essentially both this chapter and the previous chapter set out to demonstrate that this key theme is a direct consequence of the issues affecting American society at the time in which each of the texts were written. In true American Gothic style the texts studied in these last two chapters have tended to focus upon the psychological implications of cultural unease, and the manner in which this unease is reflected in the behaviours of the main characters within each text. The chapters sought to demonstrate that living with this unease will directly manifest itself in the ways in which the characters behave, and that in this respect the characters become a very real representation of and commentary upon the conditions out of which they were born.

It must not be assumed however that this representation of cultural context is an exclusively American phenomenon. Evidently there was a great deal of upheaval in American society at the time in which these texts were written and the novels are very representative of this, but in terms of offering a balanced perspective it is also necessary to explore the development of the genre on the other side of the Atlantic and look specifically to the way in which social unease is (or is not as the case may be) reflected in British works of around the same period. In order to do this, the focus of the next chapter will be to examine modern crime fiction work by a British writer, Ian Rankin and his successful series of Rebus texts.

CHAPTER FIVE

Personification and Pathetic Fallacy in Ian Rankin's *Rebus*

THE modern crime genre flourished on both sides of the Atlantic and it was during the 1980s that the number of modern crime fiction texts and the rate at which they were produced reached its peak both in Britain and in the US. There were, however, key differences within the form and style of genre as it developed in Britain and as it grew in America. In much the same way that traditional British Gothic differs from its American equivalent, so too are there distinct differences in the modern crime fiction that these two countries produced, and this chapter will look at a number of different British crime fiction texts from the 1980s and onwards as a means of understanding the ways in which the genre not only continued to develop in Britain, but also the ways in which it differed from its American contemporaries.

If we want to look a little more closely at the way in which the role of the detective and the themes of the Gothic successfully fuse in British crime writing, then we need look no further than Ian Rankin and his hugely popular detective, DI John Rebus. To date, Rankin has published 17 Rebus novels. The first (*Knots and Crosses*) appearing in 1987 (six years after *Red Dragon* and one year before *The Silence of the Lambs*), and the most recent (*Exit Music*) published in 2007. But whilst they are of the same period as the Harris texts it is here that the similarities end. They are different in a number of ways and these differences are most readily identified through the significance of location that Rankin works into in his writing and also the representation and development of character of his lead detective. Essentially Rebus combines a wonderful mixture of disgruntlement, gloom and cynicism with devotion to and determination for the job. Throughout the series Rebus himself is portrayed very much as a rough-edged diamond, a character who Rankin pitches beautifully *with* and *against* the Gothic brilliance of Edinburgh City.

Edinburgh: Multi-Layered Personality and Complex City

Throughout his 20-year span of writing, Rankin has earned himself a reputation as one of Britain's most successful crime fiction novelists, and Rebus as one of Britain's favorite fictional detectives. From the outset, Rankin identified the theme which would go on to make his work so distinctive; the Edinburgh setting and the complex relationship that Rebus has with his home city. 'There's more happening in Edinburgh than anyone knows'[159] he openly admits in *Knots and Crosses*, and this sense of there being a darker undercurrent to the city than is immediately recognisable is a theme that recurs throughout the series. Certainly Rebus appears to have a love-hate relationship with the place he calls home; at once Edinburgh is both beautiful and elegant, and yet it carries with it dark historical undertones that are deeply threatening. It is a theme that is traditionally Gothic in origin and yet one that Rankin manages to make modern by increasing the complexity of the motif; we are no longer simply contending with a single castle or two independent structures – instead we have a whole city to contend with.

Unlike many early Gothic novels and early American crime writing, Rankin is explicit and detailed with regards to the setting of his texts. The very real City of Edinburgh carries with it a gritty and urban realism that is very much a new direction for modern crime fiction and is a significant shift away from traditional Gothic writing that often deliberately provided remote, elusive or even fabricated settings through which to make their point. It is as a result of his careful representation of the city that Rankin is so able to exploit a number of traditional Gothic conventions with seeming ease. He is able to project Edinburgh as being both a veritable monster; a looming predator hiding behind a façade of tourist traps and bright lights, and a victim too – used and abused by the villainous characters that inhabit it.

This concept of there being two sides to the city is deftly revealed through the description of the castle in *The Naming of the Dead* (2005). From one perspective, the Castle takes 'on the aspect of a louring Transylvanian lair' making you 'wonder if you'd lost your colour vision' and yet when viewed from another side it is possible to climb 'a gentle slope to its entrance, with little hint of its enormous presence'.[160] By portraying the castle in this way Rankin is able to expose the deep conflict with regards to the predatory aspect that the City has and also its ability to *hide* this aspect of itself. Immediately we sense that there is a deceptive quality to the City and that it is capable of hiding its true intent and purpose. Behind the seeming beauty and grandeur there is a predator that is poised, pitched and ready to attack in an attempt to defend itself. It is a desperate indicator of both aggression and basic survival instinct that has been passed down through generation after generation that manifests itself as much in the buildings that make up the City's skyline as much as it affects the people that inhabit it.

That the City operates at a number of different levels, the visible and obvious against the hidden and the secret, is evident in the very geography of the place itself. From the exposed high peaks of the Castle, Salisbury Crags and Arthur's Seat right down to the hidden underground streets and vaults of Mary King's Close, there is always a significant sub-text within Rankin's work that there is very much more going on than meets the eye and this more often than not correlates with his multi-layered and complex physical and geographical image of the city. This ability to generate such conflict of interests and split personality is a defining feature in Rankin's work, and one that he uses to great effect to cast poignant social commentary and observation into his writing. In every single Rebus novel, without exception there is at least one reference or allusion to the dual nature of Edinburgh City, and these references always detail that despite its seemingly benign, even beautiful appearance, there is a much darker underworld at play. It is a concept succinctly revealed in the differing ways in which Jean Burchill (*The Falls* 2001) and Rebus regard the City, in that what for her is a 'beautiful city' is nothing more that 'a crime scene waiting to happen'[161] for him. The same sentiment is expressed in *Mortal Causes* (1994) too, as Father Leary states that 'that's the beauty of Edinburgh, you're never far from a peaceful spot' only to have a cynical Rebus retort that you are 'never far from a hellish one either.'[162]

To this extent the advancement that Rankin has made regarding the importance of location or of dwellings in modern crime fiction can quite clearly be seen. No longer do houses, castles, motels even, serve to be simply a physical manifestation of their owner's psychological status but instead become living and breathing characters in their own right. Rankin has personified Edinburgh to such an extent that it ceases to become just a place in the novels; we respond to it and we recognise that it needs protecting just as much as those that live in it need protecting. Resultingly the relationship between the *public* and the *private* faces of Edinburgh form a crucial part not only in authenticating the Gothic aspect of Rankin's work but also because they act as a conduit for Rankin to accommodate social observations and commentary into his texts, another way in which these novels may be interpreted as being influenced by traditional Gothic form.

Often at first glance Edinburgh is portrayed as a place to be feared, but as the novels progress it is revealed that the city also has a great deal of vulnerability about it. There is a current of tangible tension present in every novel, particularly in the latter ones, whereby Edinburgh appears to be on the brink of social collapse induced by the heavy burden of the conflict of interests that lie within it and the people that it houses. In *The Naming of the Dead* following the G8 summit it is commented that what is really needed in the area is 'the rebuilding of a shattered community'[163] and in *Fleshmarket Close* (2004) racial tensions are exposed as a result of a race murder occurring in Edinburgh's 'dumping ground'[164], the Knoxland housing scheme. It is in *Fleshmarket Close* that Rebus reflects upon the somewhat superficial vision of Edinburgh that is presented to visitors as they pass through the outskirts of the city to the city itself:

> ...bungalows fronting the route, housing schemes hidden behind them. It was the bungalows the visitors would see, Rebus realized, and they'd think what a nice, upright place Edinburgh was, the reality was waiting somewhere else, just out of their eye-line.[165]

Perhaps the most truly representative and insightful comment passed upon Edinburgh, however, is the question asked in *Doors Open* (2008); 'wasn't Edinburgh the very city that...spawned Dr. Jekyll and Mr. Hyde?'[166] Whilst *Doors Open* is not actually a Rebus novel this quote highlights perfectly the nature of split personality and of one thing being made up of two halves which is *exactly* the representation of Edinburgh that we have in the Rebus texts. Beautiful city by day, and yet a place that turns into a veritable predator after dark. It is important to remember, however, that despite the *appearance* of monstrosity the *reality* is in fact quite the opposite and it is the overall role of the city as long suffering *victim* that that forms the longest lasting impression.

Rather than being the villain of the piece, what we have in Edinburgh is a city that is revealed to be effectively the sum of its parts, both past and present, and this volatile existence whereby the city is perceived to attack and yet also to be under attack operates as a veritable embodiment of all that is wrong within it. That Rebus has deep affection for his home town is without question, but it does appear that he often struggles to understand the social changes and the self-destructive nature of the city that he recognises as being so detrimental to its overall wellbeing. There are many instances across the series where Rebus makes reference to Edinburgh's volatile past, its history as a place of rebellion, warring and bloodshed, always with the intention of suggesting that Edinburgh is a city that has always been under attack and that part of its present brutality is the direct result of having had to so consistently defend itself from invasion in the past. In *The Naming of the Dead* there is explicit reference that the city has always been 'prone to invasion'[167] and this statement could certainly be interpreted as referring as far back in time to the arrival of the Celts in Scotland or any one of the attempted invasions of the area by the Romans, Vikings or the capture of the city by the West Irish Scots. There could also be a much more modern and culturally representative interpretation, and that is the anticipated arrival (invasion to an extent) of protestors to the area in response to the G8 summit.

In *Fleshmarket Close* Rebus confides to Siobhan that he feels perpetually 'surrounded by ghosts'[168] and it is this sentiment that earmarks Rankin as one who is very skilfully able to manipulate traditional Gothic motif, implying as he does so here that one can never truly escape the past – and that the living present is often very little more than a bubble of self-fulfilled prophecy that is bound inextricably to the past. Both Rebus and Edinburgh are troubled by not only the ghosts of their past as it were, but also by the increasingly complex and perplexing demands that are made upon them by those that dwell within the city, as Rebus states in *Dead Souls* (1999):

> The years separating the present from that long-ago event seemed
> to fall away. It was as if the two could live side by side, the past a
> ghostly presence forever of the here and now. Nothing lost; nothing
> forgotten...[169]

The notion of the past as inescapable and of having direct ramifications upon the ability to be content in the present is an interesting one and certainly one that is fundamentally Gothic. Much is made throughout the Rebus series of Edinburgh's unique history, and it is this that makes it such an interesting choice of location and veritable melting-pot of conflict and contradiction. Certainly understanding, or at the very least having some knowledge of, the city's violent past is crucial in interpreting how and why the city functions as it does in the present. Through the admission that Edinburgh has a 'blood-soaked past'[170] with a history 'full of licence and riotous behaviour'[171] to the revelation that its modern day occupants 'like Edinburghers of old...could become invisible to trouble'[172] it can quite clearly be seen that Edinburgh and its citizens share a link to the past that simply cannot be ignored. Perhaps the most pertinent example of this tight link between past and present however, comes at the end of *Dead Souls* as Rebus reflects upon the state of the city that he calls home:

> No longer twilight now. Darkness had fallen. Shadows seemed to rise
> all around him as a bell tolled in the distance. The blood that had seeped
> into stone, the bones that lay twisting in their eternity, the stories and
> horrors of the city's past and present...he knew they'd all come rising in
> the digger's steel jaws, bubbling to the surface as the city began its slow
> ascent towards being a nation's capital once again.[173]

The way in which we respond and understand the city in this example is carefully manipulated by Rankin. In much the same way as Harris divulged aspects of Dolarhyde's childhood in order to evoke a degree of sympathy and pity for the reader, so too does Rankin exploit Edinburgh's past in order to construct an image of simultaneous villain and victim.

Of course Rankin is not the first Scottish writer to use a Scottish setting to expose some of the more serious social issues affecting Britain in the 1980 and early 1990s and for the most part these works are set in either Edinburgh or Scotland's other major city, Glasgow. Certainly Irvine Welsh's 1993 novel *Trainspotting*, although not a crime novel, depicts with unsparing awfulness many of the issues surrounding social, economic and political depravation in Edinburgh in the late 1980s and this same sense of hardness and meanness of streets attitude is also very much present in Glenn Chandler's Glasgow-based television series *Taggart* which first appeared on our screen in 1983 and is still running today.

Indeed the Glasgow that Jim Taggart works and lives in is without doubt a grim place, and the first ever episode *Killer* very much sets the scene for the representation of Glasgow and its citizens that recur throughout the early series. The plot in *Killer* revolves around the murders of three Glaswegian women and the subsequent investigation led by Taggart to find the killer before he or she strikes again. It is, however, through the visual images of the depravation affecting Glasgow and Scotland in the early 1980s that the true extent of the acute poverty of the area is revealed; and to this effect Glasgow is portrayed as a city of high-rises, wastelands, dank canals and disused walkways. Of course the modern *Taggart* and the representations of Glasgow that it offers is very different from these early episodes, the city has changed a great deal since the late 1970s and early 1980s and the programme reflects this, but it is the impressions cast by

these earlier episodes of the programme that most clearly reveal the significance of location in crime writing of this period, and that is the association
between urban decay and brutal crime. There is a similar level of grimness
and depravation in the portrayal of Glasgow in Craig Russell's Private
Investigator Lennox series set in the 1950s, whereby the sentiment that only
the toughest will survive is overtly clear. Just as there was in *Taggart*, in
Russell's novels too there is a strong criminal underworld at play and the
unmistakable message that there is no such thing as lady luck or Providence
anymore, and you have to be both ruthless *and* canny to survive.

There is a strong sense of the criminal underworld within Rankin's texts
too, and this underworld is given voice and face by the presence of Big Ger
Cafferty who to all extents and purposes is the driving force behind much
of Edinburgh's seedier and shadier side. What Rankin does that is so very
different from almost any other Scottish writer (or at least a writer who
locates his or her work in either of Scotland's main cities) Craig Russell,
Louise Welsh, Irvine Welsh and Glenn Chandler included, is to always
present us with an image of Edinburgh's beauty alongside its darker side so
that we constantly have the simultaneous image of beauty *and* beast in our
minds. Understanding the way in which the presence of both the beauty
and the beast combine within modern crime fiction is important to us if we
are reading Rankin as one who demonstrates significant Gothic leaning in
his work.

In presenting Edinburgh both as villain *and* victim, as a place consumed
by both desire *and* suffering, Rankin is able to make a huge leap forward in
the complexity of status of location in modern crime fiction. In his work the
city becomes not just a physical metaphor to reflect the mindset of the
villain, as was the chief intent in early Gothic writing; essentially it is the
villain, and of course the ultimate victim too. Resultingly the role Edinburgh
holds within the texts is of supreme importance and Edinburgh as setting
becomes an absolutely integral part of Rankin's writing. To prove the point,
one only has to ask oneself if the stories would work if they were set, in say
Norwich? Or would Rebus himself be such a plausible character had he
hailed from Torquay? The answer to both, of course, is no. In exploiting the
history of Edinburgh and its people Rankin is able to introduce the complex
theme of psycho-geography, specifically the way in which people relate to
places, into his texts. Because Edinburgh is a city with such strength of
character and history it cannot help but influence and guide (both actually
and metaphorically) those characters that weave their way through the
narrative and resultingly the moral issues that Rebus has to deal with (the
secrets, hypocrisies, social intricacies, flaws, failure and victories) are not

only *his* moral issues, but Edinburgh's too. The city's contradictory and perplexing make up is very much a part of Rebus' psyche and the novels are, as much as their author, resolutely Scottish.

Rebus as Detective

If it is true that Rankin makes such significant advancement within the genre in terms of the increased complexity and importance of location, are we to assume that the same is true of the representation of the detective within his novels? Certainly Rebus is not the first fictional detective to appear in more than one text and to have his character developed across an entire series, but the extent to which this happens within Rankin's work *is* worthy of serious attention. To have the same detective reappear across a number of different crime stories has been a feature of detective fiction as far back as Poe's Dupin and Conan Doyle's Holmes. It was a trend that continued into Golden Age writing (Christie's Miss Marple and Hercule Poirot and Sayers' Lord Peter Wimsey for example) and was also a feature of much American Hard-Boiled writing (Daly's Race Williams and Chandler's Philip Marlowe).

Whilst the advantages of developing consistency of character across an entire series of texts may be obvious (certainly it makes for fluency and fluidity across the texts, giving the reader a degree of faith and sure footing behind the upheaval and uncertainty that revolves around the actual crime itself, not to mention the increased marketing opportunities generated by the development of a serial detective), it is the way in which Rankin unites his serial detective Rebus with his serial setting of Edinburgh that is such a defining feature of his work. As a location we come to understand the city and to relate to it just as much as we do Rebus himself. Whilst it is true that within the Gothic and the move from the Gothic into crime fiction, setting has always been important, the degree to which Rebus and Edinburgh are ultimately bound to each other is very much a new direction for modern crime fiction.

Rebus shares features of both the Golden Age detective and the Hard-Boiled detective, and before beginning to look at the relationship he has with the city within the novels it is necessary to analyse who and what he is in himself. Raised in Scotland at a time in which heavy industry was in rapid decline and career opportunities were severely limited, Rebus is portrayed as a stereotypical Scottish hard man. He is a loner, a heavy drinker and a heavy smoker who finds it hard to maintain personal relationships. He has an innate desire to rebel against authority as much as he can within the boundaries of his profession and seems always to have his finger hovering over the self-destruct button, without ever managing to push on it sufficiently to bring about his ruin. Despite this, or maybe because of it, he is an intensely likeable character whose loyalty to those he likes and respects, and to the city and its people that he protects, is absolutely without question.

Cynical and disgruntled, he is very much aware of the fact that crime in his city will never go away, but nevertheless believes that his job does allow him to make a difference, albeit small, to those people that he comes into contact with. It is this concept of Edinburgh as having flaws and vices that will never be eradicated that essentially forms the bond between him and his home city; whilst Edinburgh refuses to come under police control and to lose its vices, so too does Rebus refuse to be bound totally by the rules that govern him and let go of *his* vices. In this respect the tie between Rebus and Edinburgh becomes clear, and because Rankin has personified the city to such an extent, it is a relationship that we can believe. Together they provide purpose for each other and because Rankin has invested such time and detail into developing and building them both up across the series we as reader are able to see beyond and behind the flaws in each and respond to them appropriately.

It is a very different technique to that applied by Harris to generate sympathy and understanding for his detectives across his Lecter series. Whereas Harris placed a greater emphasis upon developing the personal history of his detectives (Graham and Starling, though it is to Starling that the greatest detail is given), Rankin links Rebus and Edinburgh to such an extent that Rebus' personal history is revealed through the city's history and effectively they become the same. This degree of personification and psychological tying together of people and places is representative of yet another step forward in developing and sustaining the character of the detective.

Like Harris, Rankin is also keen to move away from seeming simplicity within the detective genre and the concept of a 'detective' story, whereby his 'crime' writing is definitive only by the level of and type of crime that it portrays. Certainly in a great many of the latter novels, and by this I mean those where Rankin has moved away from the theme of game play and gamesmanship that characterised those early novels (*Knots and Crosses, Hide and Seek* and *Strip Jack*), a greater degree of complexity is present and there are often several plots in operation at the same time. In keeping with the realities of the setting and of modern day policing, Rebus and his colleagues are often involved in more than one investigation or case at a time. It is in these latter texts that the actual crime within the novel becomes almost secondary to the overall message of the novel as a whole and this relates less to the solving of the crime(s) per se and more to the exposure of acute problems of the society in which the crimes have occurred. Within a great many of the Rebus texts there is a great emphasis placed upon calling into question a much deeper understanding of the *real* crime that has befallen Edinburgh, and that is not the rapes, thefts or murders that the stories are about, but instead it is the ultimate chaos and veritable *undoing* of society that the crimes cause.

Arguably the Edinburgh that Rebus resides in is an example of a society that lacks cohesion and direction and this lack manifests itself in the behaviour of those who reside in the city, specifically the victims and the villains that we are introduced to. The concept of society and all that it represents is undoubtedly broken, and it is this that appears to be the *real crime* behind the texts; the detrimental and yet seemingly inevitable result of a society that has effectively (through a number of different ways) brought about its own downfall.

If we are looking towards the representation of Edinburgh as part-victim and part-villain then it is necessary also to look also to the roles of other victims and other villains present within the texts. Certainly within the realistic gritty and urban setting that Edinburgh provides it is no longer safe to assume that victims are as innocent or indeed that villains are simply as guilty as they were in traditional Gothic writing. Perhaps the most pertinent example of this shift in the questionable innocence of victims is evident in the issues that are raised in Rankin's sixth Rebus novel *Mortal Causes*. Set against the fun and frivolity of the Edinburgh Festival Rankin quickly turns our attention to the discovery of a tortured body left hanging in a vaulted room beneath the streets of the city centre.

In the first instance our pity is aroused by the very graphic prologue that Rankin provides us with before the true identity of the victim is revealed in a later chapter. Flashbacks of the victim's childhood reveal to us that he was 'cherished and abandoned in equal measure', distanced from his father and witness to his mother's despair. The victim was involved in gangs, the initiation into which took place when he was thirteen and the knuckle skinning that formed part of this dreadful rite of passage 'hurt until he belonged.'[174] Sympathy at this point for sure, but when we finally learn that the victim is none other than Cafferty's son, whose links to terrorism and Northern Ireland jeopardise the safety of not only Edinburgh's citizens but also of those tourists here for the Festival, it is a sympathy that begins to waver. Of course not all of the victims across the series have brought about their own downfall in the way that Cafferty's son has and the vast majority of them *are* innocent victims of abhorrent crimes, but what this example does show us is that within Rankin's work it is no longer safe to *assume* that just because one is a victim that one is entirely innocent also.

If we recognise that there is a difference in the way in which the role of victim has changed then perhaps also there is scope to assess whether the role of villain has changed too, and indeed it has. Whereas the earlier examples of crime fiction referred to have placed a great deal of emphasis upon detailing the personal histories of the villains (with particular weighting upon their childhoods), with the purpose of providing some degree of psychological insight into the motivations for the crimes, this aspect of understanding is notably absent from Rankin's work. Because it is such a glaring difference we need to ask what the reasons might be behind this very different approach to understanding motivations and the point that Rankin is trying to make as a result of this absence. Unlike Bloch and Harris who reference so explicitly the significant aspects of their villains' childhoods in order that the reader may begin to form a degree of understanding (and by the term 'understanding' I mean exactly that; understanding is not akin to the provision of excuses for their behaviour nor is it to be interpreted as a means of absolving them of their guilt), Rankin gives his villains no such 'get out of jail free' card.

In a style more akin to that of John Fowles' 1963 text *The Collector*, Rankin's villains are mostly motivated by greed, jealousy, money or the desire to keep a secret hidden that equates to selfishness. They are not faceless beings ignored by society, nor are they revealed to be deeply troubled individuals consumed and thwarted by unresolved issues of identity. What they represent instead is nothing other than modern society in which moral values are questionable, and in which culpability and responsibility are largely absent. The result of this is that society has, to a large extent become soulless. With this in mind our response Rebus' seeming disgruntlement and resentment is much easier to understand as it is increasingly he and his colleagues who are left to sweep up the pieces of this broken city. It is a thankless task, and one in which Rebus essentially is set up to fail; the rapes, the murders and the burglaries are the mere tip of the iceberg. The gloom and doom that pervades so many of the texts is indeed a manifestation of the despair of the city and its inhabitants who have no chance of salvation until what is wrong at the core of the city is repaired.

The Scottish Condition and English Equivalents

In attributing many of the darker themes and tones to Rankin's work to the 'Scottish Condition' of the 1980–90s, it would surely be interesting to compare the way in which society is portrayed in English crime writing of around the same period, and for this I intend to examine some of works by Ruth Rendell (Chief Inspector Wexford) and Colin Dexter (Detective Chief Inspector Morse). Although both of these detectives were created before the 1980s and continued to appear in novels well into the 90s (and beyond in the case of Wexford) they were both active in the same period as the Rankin novels began to appear and it is because of this that comparison between them is relevant.

If we consider in the first instance the settings and locations in which Wexford and Morse operate, the first of many differences between these two English writers and the Scottish writing of Rankin becomes apparent. Certainly the fictional town of Kingsmarkham (Wexford) and the very real city of Oxford (Morse) differ greatly from the brutal realism of Rankin's Edinburgh. Whilst it is true that Kingsmarkham is a far cry from picture postcard representation of a small English town (it does after all come with housing estates, wastelands, vandalised bus shelters and a sprawling multi-storey car park or two). It certainly has sufficient pleasant countryside surrounding it and an air of gentility about it to make us realise that we are indeed reading a very different kind of detective novel to that typified by Ian Rankin; certainly Kingsmarkham could never be referred to as the 'beast'[175] that Edinburgh is.

There are significant differences too between the protagonists of each series; Rebus is a detective who is willing to follow his own instincts and operate outside of protocol, Wexford is one who plays by the book and follows procedure. Whereas Rebus is often perceived as unapproachable and of having difficulty maintaining personal relationships, Wexford is much more stable and grounded. What both of these detectives are, however, is entirely suited to the areas in which they operate. Although Wexford is not necessarily a *product* of his environment in the way that Rebus is, he is very much at one with Kingsmarkham and is exactly the type of affable, considerate and middle-class detective that one would expect to find within such an area. This same degree of affinity between detective and place can be seen in Colin Dexter's portrayal of *his* fictional detective, Detective Chief Inspector Morse. Set in the historical, affluent, literary and cultured city of Oxford we were never going to find a Rebus-esque detective operating within Dexter's novels. To the contrary and rather appropriately, what we have in Morse is a suitably educated and cultured officer, effectively the human equivalent of the city in which he works. From his taste in classical music and opera to the car that he drives (a Lancia in Dexter's texts, a Mark 2 Jaguar in the television series) he, like both Rebus and Wexford, is suited entirely to his environment.

To have detectives educationally and culturally appropriate to their environments and to the crimes that they investigate is not a new feature of detective fiction, or indeed of modern crime fiction. Agatha Christie's seemingly benign Miss Marple hails from the apparently quaint and genteel St. Mary Mead – a place whose peaceful appearance belies the capability of its inhabitants to commit all manner of crimes in much the same way that Marple's apparent frailty and reserve belies an acute shrewdness. Likewise the detectives and private eyes of hard-boiled detective fiction are often just as hardened and worldly wise as the cities in which they live and work.

There are exceptions to this rule however, and one of the few writers *not* to follow this trend whereby the character traits of the detective are synonymous with the character traits of the environments in which they operate is P.D. James and her fictional detective, Commander Adam Dalgleish. In terms of sensitivity and intellectual interests, Dalgleish and Rebus are very many miles apart. Whilst they are both very private people, (Dalgleish's interest in poetry and his supreme sense of self-control set him apart so significantly from Rebus) what they do share is a base in a bustling city that manifests itself very differently within each of them. In Dalgleish's capacity as a Commander however, he is frequently taken out of London and it is this that prevents him from having the fundamental link to his 'home' environment that the other officers demonstrate. Because he is the only one of the four detectives referred to here that moves away from his primary location (London) so frequently, he simply cannot be said to be so closely linked to his environment as each of the other detectives. Of course there are a great many of the novels that *are* set in London (*A Certain Justice*, *Original Sin* and *The Murder Room* to name a few), but equally there are many in which Dalgleish is required to leave London (*Devices and Desires*, *Death in Holy Orders* and *The Lighthouse* amongst others). That he travels out of the city so much effectively means that he simply cannot be seen to be a part of it in the same way in which the other detectives are a part of theirs.

There are also differing extents to which each of these British authors relies upon aspects of the Gothic to add subtext or enhance the effect of their writing. We have seen already how Rankin, particularly when it comes to setting, readily and consistently exploits Gothic motif to give credence to the concept of Edinburgh as a brooding monster. He is able to deftly link *environment* to *psychological status* in a style that was evident in the Gothic as far back as Horace Walpole's text, and it is interesting that by and large this is something that is avoided by the English writers mentioned in this chapter thus far.

This absence of Gothic motif within the English examples is such a different approach to Rankin's writing that it needs analysing in greater detail if we are to understand why it occurs. To recap hereto it has been suggested that many of the earliest Gothic texts used the Gothic genre as a means of making poignant social and political observations linked to the period in which they were written. Growing out of this genre was the earliest form of detective fiction which used aspects of the Gothic to inject suspense, mystery and unease into the narrative whilst continuing the theme of social observation that formed such a strong part of early Gothic writing. Whilst it is true that detective fiction *can* operate without the Gothic, what detective texts of this type lack that their Gothic influenced counterparts do not, is significant social commentary. Thus Rankin with his heavy Gothic influence can be categorized as a writer of modern crime fiction who comprises social observation, Gothic motif and a detective element; those writers that do not make use of the Gothic are defined as writers of detective fiction rather than writers of modern crime fiction and make little reference to social context. This is not to say however that no social speculation occurs within the detective fiction of English writers, or that the Gothic is *always* eliminated from their writing. Crime cannot be reported or recorded in any way without some reference to the context out of which it has arisen, but what it does means is that the social aspect to these detective novels is not as heavily weighted as it is in examples of genuine modern crime fiction.

The Significance of Social Context: Immigration and Racial Tension in Rankin's *Fleshmarket Close* and Ruth Rendell's *Simisola*

Throughout this chapter only fleeting reference has been made to the way in which Rankin includes significant *actual* social context and actual social events into his work. *The Naming of the Dead* is pitched against the G8 summit that took place in Scotland in 2005, the brutality of the crime in *Mortal Causes* is set against the frivolity of the annual Edinburgh Festival and in

Fleshmarket Close Rankin gives voice and perspective to the very real issue of illegal immigrants in Scotland and the racist fury that this can ignite.

Another author who offers social insight in her work is Ruth Rendell, and it is interesting to compare the ways in which the themes of racial tension and immigration are handled in Rankin's *Fleshmarket Close* and Rendell's 1994 novel *Simisola*. From the outset there are stark differences in the tone of the texts; *Fleshmarket Close* opens at the Knoxland housing scheme, the walls of which have been grafittied heavily with explicit racist messages, and *Simisola* begins at the seemingly innocuous Kingsmarkham GP Surgery. Like so much of Rankin's work the tensions at play within Edinburgh are treated with harsh brutality by the author, and he never presents the city as anything other than what it is. Its flaws, alongside its beauty are constantly revealed to us and form a crucial part of the text. Rendell's Kingsmarkham on the other hand, behind its seeming gentility and gentleness, is rarely all that it appears, or claims to be. Whereas Rankin introduces his theme to us bluntly and from page one, Rendell prefers to drip feed us into the real subtext of the novel, slowly introducing the theme of racism into the text. Because it is introduced so slowly the notion that racist tensions even exist in Kingsmarkham comes as an uncomfortable surprise to many of the characters in the text, Wexford himself included here, and the detective finds himself forced to take an introspective look at himself and question prejudices and ignorances that he did not even know that he had.

The most blatant example of this ignorance is the shocking misidentification of a young black woman's body for that of missing black girl Melanie Akande. Following the mistake Wexford admits that 'it had shown him he was wrong about himself' and that it 'had occurred through prejudice, through racism, through making an assumption he could never have made if the missing girl were white and the body white.'[176] Rebus on the other hand could never be accused of making such a mistake; he is very much aware (much more so that Wexford) of his own fallibility, his own weariness of the world and of the problems caused by immigration and the racial tension that it brings, especially to a place like Knoxland. So in tune is he with Edinburgh and all of its social problems that seldom is anything a true surprise or shock to him any more, and because he has seen it all before there is very little need to jump to any form of conclusion in the way that Wexford did. Indeed there is perhaps some evidence that Rebus even expected a crime of this nature to happen in Edinburgh soon as he fails to contradict journalist Steve Holly's statement it was 'only a matter of time before *we* had one.'[177]

That Rebus is more in tune with his working environment than Wexford becomes obvious when we compare the texts in this way, but this is not meant in any way to be a slight upon Wexford's character; to the contrary he is a good man who will undoubtedly learn from his mistake. What it does do is demonstrate the deep flaws hidden far beneath the surface of white middle-class England and it is this realisation that earmarks Kingsmarkham as altogether a different type of monster than Edinburgh city.

Of course as the novels develop it becomes apparent that although each novel undoubtedly addresses notions of racism, the motivations for the murders in each text are very different. Both of these novels demonstrate the increasing tendency within modern crime fiction (Rankin) and detective fiction (Rendell) for murder to be treated with a degree of flippancy that is distinctly different from the sheer desire for survival that was typical of early Gothic writing and also the examples of American crime writing (Bloch and Harris) that have been described in previous chapters. For Manfred, just as for Bates, Dolarhyde and Gumb, desire (and the crime that this desire generated) was an absolute necessity and integral to survival. That is not to excuse their behaviour, just to demonstrate that the motivations behind the crimes of these characters were fundamentally different to the motivations behind the rationale for the crimes in the Rankin and Rendell texts, whereby murder is presumed by the perpetrators to be a justifiable means for achieving personal wants. There is also great variation within the theme of social context and the ways in which it is represented within these two texts (Rankin in particular) and examples of the modern crime fiction of Thomas Harris (*Dragon* and *Silence*). The Harris texts made bold comments with regard to the failings and of a number of different institutions put in place to protect their citizens, but it was all done through metaphor and allusion. Rankin however, uses no such disguise, and the exasperations and frustrations that he feels in failing to apprehend the criminals quickly are explicitly detailed.

Social commentary regarding paranoia and institutional failure form a large part of Harris' main plot and well as his sub-plots, but unlike Rankin and Rendell who make similarly pertinent social observations in *their* writing, the exact nature of this commentary is never actually specified and is only evident within the metaphorical reading and interpretation of the Gothic aspects of the texts. Resultingly the reader is compelled to consider the differing agendas behind the novels of Rankin and Harris and recognise that there is a different purpose to the writings of each. Rankin's texts are more predictable and realistic in the issues that they tackle (given their location within a modern city centre); we can expect to find within them issues such as racial tension, drug and alcohol abuse, violence and rape because these are the issues that we expect to find happening within a city centre. In contrast there is no such degree of predictability within Harris' texts, and the nature of and the meaning behind the crimes only become understandable when we understand the social context out of which they have arisen. Harris it seems has a very clear purpose in his writing, and that is to expose the consequences of such a unique period in American history and to this extent the nature of the crimes that he details are suitably unique. Rankin's purpose it seems is to expose the innate difficulties of modern city living, and the crimes that occur within *his* texts fit this agenda too.

CHAPTER SIX

Le Loup-Garou en Amerique: European Influence and Gothic Traditionalism in Patricia Cornwell's *Black Notice*, *The Last Precinct* and *Blow Fly*

O F course Edinburgh with its grisly past and Gothic associations makes a wonderful setting for any type of crime or detective story. What makes Rankin's work so unique and in turn so appropriate for inclusion in this text is the juxtaposition between the historical aspect of Edinburgh city and the very modern depiction of society and crime that Rankin presents us with. Throughout the series this conflict between old and new remains constant and understanding this relationship becomes pivotal in recognising not only the inherent problems within Edinburgh city itself, but also how the Gothic continues to effectively influence modern crime fiction.

Another writer to do this to great effect is the American author Patricia Cornwell, whose Scarpetta series provides an excellent example of the way in which traditional European Gothic can fuse with a smaller sub-genre of modern crime fiction that is recognisable by its heavy emphasis upon forensics and the important role that forensic assessment has in identification and apprehension of the criminal(s). Throughout the Scarpetta series Cornwell uses a range of Gothic techniques to achieve a number of effects and meanings, some more successful than others, but the texts that exploit this most effectively are those in the wonderfully indulgent Chandonne trilogy (*Black Notice*, *The Last Precinct* and *Blow Fly*), and it is on these texts specifically that this chapter will focus.

In terms of writing prowess, Cornwell is without question one of the most successful and most prolific crime writers around. Her style of writing is one that the market place now calls serial killer fiction and Cornwell is credited with having established 'a small sub-genre within serial killer fiction – the professional female pathologist/forensic psychiatrist/criminologist tale of detection'[178]. Since the first Kay Scarpetta novel *Postmortem* appeared in 1990, Cornwell has produced 17 further novels in the series, each one a best-seller both here and in the US. In a competitive field, Cornwell has certainly proved that she has staying power as a master of her genre, but what can we make of her writing and her story telling ability that *justifies* her place amongst the modern literary elite? Certainly Cornwell demonstrates marked talent when it comes to writing successful crime fiction. Her ability to combine enough soap opera style melodrama to make her novels appeal to the mass market whilst at the same time incorporating intrinsic forensic detail that is largely led by a female protagonist was a unique approach back in the early 1990s when her novels first started to appear. Her approach has given her a huge following as a writer of modern crime fiction, but it has earned her harsh criticism too, especially with regards to the perceived predictability and formulaic nature of some of her plots.

Gothic Flair

Whilst it is true that there is a degree of autonomy of plot within her novels and that many of her characters appear to be larger than life parodies of good and evil, it depends how much of a fan of traditional Gothic writing you are as to whether this tendency is in any way detrimental to her work. If we are to credit this author as one who successfully presents a very modern day take upon traditional Gothic writing then we should expect there to be some degree of formula within her writing and stereotyping to her characters because this is essentially what the Gothic entails. It is of course Cornwell's standing as a writer who *is* able to manipulate the Gothic and to incorporate traditional Gothic convention into her work that makes her such a suitable candidate for inclusion in this text.

If we look at the Scarpetta series as a whole, then we are able to see from the outset the way in which Cornwell adopts Gothic motif into her writing. First and foremost must be considered the battle between good and evil that represents the struggle for justice within each of her novels, and struggle is very much a part of Cornwell's first Scarpetta novel *Postmortem*. In this example the perpetrator, Roy McCorkle, is strangling women in Richmond and Scarpetta must use all her wits and expertise in order to catch him and stop the killing. In this respect it is quite easy to see how this particular novel functions to introduce Scarpetta in her role as the potential heroine of the piece and set her up against the force of evil (McCorkle in this case, but the pattern is repeated throughout the series) whoever it may be. Although in this text Scarpetta does not come under direct attack from McCorkle himself and she is never actually personally threatened by him (this type of persecution by the offender will become a feature in later novels), it is easy to see Cornwell constructing the role of Gothic heroine for Kay Scarpetta in this opening example. Not only is she (Scarpetta) pitched against McCorkle in an attempt to restore safety and security to the women of Virginia and find justice for those victims he has already claimed, she also finds herself under persecution and attack from Amburgey, Marino and to a lesser extent the rather obnoxious 10-year-old Lucy.

Indeed the way in which Scarpetta increasingly becomes a hounded heroine within the texts will very much become a stock theme as the series progresses and she begins to find herself matched against increasingly dangerous and damaging attacks (both personally and professionally) from those around her. This is a theme which peaks in Cornwell's pivotal eleventh Scarpetta novel, *The Last Precinct*, (to be examined in closer detail later in this chapter) which sees her professional and personal statuses changed irrecoverably. In understanding and accepting that Scarpetta does indeed hold the role of heroine within the texts, becoming a physical representation of the force of good that faces a daily struggle against those who attempt to undermine her, we can begin to understand the way in which Cornwell has constructed her lead character based upon the traditional Gothic heroine. Scarpetta, like Isabella, Ellena, Mina Harker and Clarice Starling, must face her demons, in whatever shape or form they take, in order to emerge victorious.

Cornwell's villains are similarly constructed, and in a great number of texts there is distinct Gothic influence in the ways in which the villains or evil forces within the texts are constructed and portrayed. That so many of Cornwell's villains seem to possess such strong Gothic influence is something that has attracted much critical attention in the past, and appraisals of Cornwell's work have criticised her technique, stating that 'at her worst [Cornwell] plunges into melodrama and gothic excess, especially in the depiction of her archvillains.'[179] That this tendency to incorporate the Gothic into her work is perceived as being detrimental to its quality and overall effect is something that I have to disagree with and certainly may have much to do with the perception and interpretation of Cornwell's fiction as being simply a 'reworking of the genre of crime fiction'[180], rather than it being a reworking of the Gothic. Certainly the chief motivation behind *this* text has been to argue and demonstrate the ways in which modern crime fiction is beholden to the Gothic, suggesting that it could simply not exist without demonstrating both an understanding of the Gothic form and also adhering to its formulaic constraints. Cornwell's writing, complete with its heavy Gothic influence is indeed a perfect example of how this works.

Of course Cornwell's perpetrators and the ways in which they are depicted are very much a defining aspect of her work and her critics make accurate assessment; a great many of them *are* constructed from traditional Gothic villains. Many of them possess physical oddities; the albino Temple Brooks Gault, the 'midget' Oscar Bane, the genetically defective Roy McCorkle, the scar-faced Newton Joyce and the hypertrichosis afflicted Jean-Baptiste Chandonne are striking examples of this tendency and pattern in her novels. That it is such a repeated pattern and such a defining feature of her novels certainly supports the notion that there is indeed a case for defining the villain in Cornwell's work as 'THE MONSTER'[181] rather than simply the *criminal* or the *perpetrator* because they do very often tend to be "abnormal' in the psychological sense of the term, but often also in the physical one.'[182] Certainly the extent to which this assessment it a true reflection of the role that the villain holds within the texts will become apparent when we look to the 'monster' that stalks the pages of *Black Notice*, *The Last Precinct* and *Blow Fly* – the monstrous Jean-Baptiste Chandonne.

That her killers should possess such abnormalities is a significant aspect to her work; in order for Cornwell to truly capture Gothic sentiment it is *imperative* that she present her villains, or forces of evil, as profoundly different to the way in which she presents her forces of good. By doing this she can create a definite sense of 'otherness' for her villains that separate them distinctly from the rest of society. It is our understanding and our response to the 'other' that defines the way in which we respond to her texts; that we are both simultaneously fascinated and appalled by her creations is an effect only achieved by creating sub-human 'others' that are capable of destruction of society on a whim.

The representation of the 'outsider' in literature and other forms of media is a well-researched field, and there is much written that addresses specifically the way in which the 'archetypal outsider'[183] in popular culture is constructed. Whilst it is relatively easy to understand that 'the strangely formed body has represented absolute Otherness in all times and places since human history began'[184], it is perhaps less easy to understand the implication of this within modern crime fiction. However, in accepting that it is inevitable that the 'other' (or that which is alien to us in society) is, by nature of its 'otherness' that which we are most frightened of, the logic behind Cornwell's representing her villains as in some way apart from or 'other' than us should become clear. Certainly when faced with such freakery as the 'other' represents, our senses of anxiety and speculation are aroused, resulting in a 'profound disquiet that stems from being confronted by those beings that differ so greatly from that which we have come to recognize as 'normal' in appearance'[185]. In light of this to find such physical representations of 'otherness' (in the form of the villains) in Cornwell's work is unsurprising; quite simply we *are* supposed to fear her perpetrators and we should be afraid to look upon them because they intend to do us harm.

There are however exceptions to this rule and it would be a mistake and an underestimation of Cornwell's abilities as a writer to ignore the fact that there are also a great many of her villains who do *not* fit nicely under the umbrella of 'freakery'. Indeed it seems that for every physically abnormal killer there is, there is also one whose appearance is normal, allowing him or her to blend into society unnoticed. Carrie Grethen is one such example, as is Jay Talley, the sculpted Adonis and twin brother of physical freak Jean-Baptiste Chandonne. That Talley should be so deceptive in appearance is something that continuously antagonises and frustrates Jean-Baptiste, who believes Talley to be so much worse than himself because of his deceptive appearance in that he simply 'does not look like what he is.'[186]

Whilst it is true that there is strong Gothic trace throughout much of Cornwell's writing, it is in her Chandonne trilogy (*Black Notice*, *The Last Precinct* and *Blow Fly*) that her flare for the Gothic is truly indulged, and it is to these three texts that this chapter shall move to next, examining firstly the role that *Black Notice* holds as the opening text to this mini-series. By looking at this text in this way we should begin to build a definitive under-standing of the way in which Cornwell uses and manipulates traditional Gothic motif and the way in which she continues this trend into the other two texts that complete the Chandonne trilogy.

Gothic Excess in *Black Notice*

Originally published in 1999, *Black Notice* is the tenth Scarpetta novel in the series. It follows on from *Point of Origin* and begins almost a year to the day that Benton Wesley, Scarpetta's lover and FBI profiler, was murdered by Carrie Grethen and Newton Joyce. The novel opens with a letter from

Benton to Scarpetta that he wrote before his death urging her to begin to deal with her grief following his death and to begin to live her life again. The letter is brief and its meaning simple, but by placing it at the front of the novel, this seemingly innocuous letter becomes important for two reasons. Firstly it serves to remind us of Scarpetta's vulnerability, showing her as and cementing her role as victim or wounded heroine from the outset, and secondly because it sets Benton up as an omnipresent influence, a quasi-hero ('quasi' in the sense that he cannot be a true hero because at this point we, and Scarpetta, believe him to be dead) who will seek to protect and comfort her even from beyond the grave.

That the 'ghost' of Benton is so strongly felt from the beginning is certainly an important factor in the novel; even in death he is trying to engineer for himself the role of Gothic hero in that by means of this letter he is able to come to Scarpetta's aid and try to begin the process of saving her from herself. Of course it is only in *Blow Fly* that we learn that Benton is in fact not dead at all, and that his murder was an FBI cover up designed to save not only his own life, but also the lives of those closest to him. His reappearance before Scarpetta at the end of *Blow Fly*, coming as it does at the very point at which Scarpetta's reserves of mettle and determination have almost run out, essentially seals for him the role of Gothic hero that began with the letter that formed the prologue to *Black Notice*.

In its capacity as the opener to this mini-series *Black Notice* must sow the seeds and set the stage for the themes and events that will unfold in the following two texts. Effectively it has a job to do and this is perhaps why this text in particular is the most heavily Gothic of the three. There are a number of different ways in which the text can be defined as being essentially a Gothic novel and none of them are subtle. Each of them is, however, vital to recognising the relentless, systematic and absolute destruction of Scarpetta that is the core of the texts and of her ultimate rescue and the restoration of Benton to her that is the point at which *Blow Fly* ends and the series closes.

Within the text the deliberate destruction of Scarpetta becomes such a strong theme that the murders of Container Man (Thomas Chandonne) and Diane Bray are almost secondary considerations to the story. In her desire to present Scarpetta as victim, Cornwell pushes the murders to one side and much of the story-line details the constant barrage of attacks that Scarpetta endures rather than the specifics of the hunt for Chandonne's killer. So unrelenting are the attacks upon Scarpetta that the extent of her despair and isolation is revealed to us at a number of points and it becomes impossible not to recognise her standing as Gothic heroine within the narrative. She readily admits to feeling alone, but perhaps the most revealing confession occurs in France, when she states:

> I felt awful. My soul was bruised. I felt as alone as I'd ever felt in my life, as if I didn't exist, as if I were part of another person's bad dream.[187]

Of course her feelings of isolation stem not only from the professional undermining that has occurred as a result of interference masterminded by Diane Bray, but also as a result of the personal distance that she feels from Lucy, Marino and the physical absence of Benton from her life. Tied into this is the bizarre request from Interpol for her to visit France, and the deep suspicion that she is being used by Interpol as some sort of pawn and being asked to do things that may jeopardise her entire career even further. It is a series of attacks that is excessive to say the least, and quite frankly the relentless battering that Scarpetta endures is much more than one woman could be expected to withstand. Nevertheless, in her capacity as Gothic heroine it is something that she *must* withstand if she is to fulfil the role and emerge triumphant and rewarded at the end of the trilogy.

In recognising that this excess and exaggeration is an integral part of the Gothic genre, it becomes apparent that *Black Notice* is no exception to this Gothic trend despite it appearing in print some 200 years after the first Gothic novel. If the onslaught that Scarpetta faces seems beyond the limits of plausibility and excessive to the extreme then that it because it is and because it has to be, for without it the novel would cease to function as a Gothic text. Scarpetta's role as heroine would be compromised and the return of Benton at the end of it all, which is only believable within the very wide parameters of fancy that Gothic convention permits, would lose all credibility.

With this is mind then, to what extent does Jean-Baptiste Chandonne meet the criteria for Gothic villain and is his construction similarly excessive in its Gothic characteristics? The answer to this question is yes – in terms of villain, they don't come much more Gothic than Chandonne himself. Part werewolf, part vampire and part human psychopath he embodies evil at its most absolute:

> He is hideous, his face formed of two halves set together unevenly, one eye lower than the other, teeth widely spaced, small and pointed like an animal's. His entire body is covered with long, unpigmented, baby-fine hair, but it is his eyes that disturb me most. I saw hell in that stare, a lust that seemed to light up the air...[188]

It is almost impossible to picture the deformed Chandonne without being reminded of the similarly disfigured Gothic monster Quasimodo from Victor Hugo's *Notre-Dame de Paris*. Indeed it is a comparison that we are invited to make as Scarpetta describes Chandonne as a 'Quasimodo of sorts who spent his life hidden in the basement of his powerful family's Paris home.'[189] If this sounds a little far-fetched, compare the previous quotation with one taken from Hugo's *Notre-Dame de Paris*:

> In fact this little monster (we ourselves should be hard put to it to describe him otherwise) was no newborn babe. It was a very angular, very restless small mass...The head was very deformed. All you could see was the thick of red hair, an eye, a mouth, and some teeth. The eye was weeping, the mouth crying, and the teeth seemed only to want something to bite.[190]

Certainly Chandonne's appearance seems to cement his place as both a credible and a memorable Gothic monster and it is interesting to draw comparison between Hugo's Paris born 'monkey gone wrong'[191] and Cornwell's Paris born *'espéce de sale gorille'*[192].

Terrifying in his appearance, the threat that Chandonne poses whilst he remains free to kill is made even more terrifying by that fact that despite numerous references and hints of the supernatural, Chandonne is simply human – nothing more, nothing less, as Scarpetta stresses: '...he didn't step from the pages of a Mary Shelley. Chandonne is real'[193] Lest we as reader get carried away with notions of Gothic monsters or of supernatural beings released from the gates of hell and begin to forget that Jean-Baptiste is fundamentally flesh and bone just like the rest of us, Cornwell ensures that she constantly reminds us of his human status by locating a significant proportion of the text in his home country of France, his home city of Paris and even taking Scarpetta to the gates of his childhood home.

So what then are we to make of the Gothic hero within the text, and upon whom should this worthy crown be placed? With Benton gone the position needs to be filled (albeit only temporarily) and throughout the course of the novel both Marino and Lucy becomes possible contenders for the role, although for a number of different reasons neither manages to meet the required criteria for Gothic hero successfully.

Marino's failure to act as hero within the novels stems ultimately from his being simply not good enough for Scarpetta, be it physically or personally. Throughout the series Cornwell has carefully constructed Marino's position as thwarted suitor for Scarpetta's affections, and his feelings for Scarpetta are something that she is acutely aware of:

> His attention wanders around and it seeps into my awareness that he
> has never been inside my bedroom. I don't want to imagine his fantasies.
> I have known him for many years and have always been aware that his
> respect for me is potently laced with insecurity and sexual attraction. He
> is a hulk of a man with a swollen beer belly, and a big disgruntled face,
> and his hair is colorless and has unattractively migrated from his head to
> other parts of his body. I listen to my niece on the phone as Marino's eyes
> feel their way around my private space: my dressers, my closet, the open
> drawers, what I am packing, and my breasts."[194]

Certainly Marino's interest in Scarpetta is sexual, but it would be wrong to assume that this is his only feeling for her. It is not simply that he lusts for her; he does care deeply for her as we realise when he confronts Benton with the danger that he perceives Scarpetta to be in: 'Not just any doctor. We're talking about Scarpetta!'[195] It is easy to feel a certain amount of pity for Marino as he struggles to do what he believes to be right by Scarpetta. He is painfully aware of the fact that she has never had and never will have interest in him that goes beyond the platonic and the professional, and yet his feelings for her demand that he must try to help her in any way that he can, even if it means attempting to restore Benton to her and effectively shooting himself in the foot by doing so. This is not to say that were Benton to remain out of the picture, so to speak, he and Scarpetta would have any future together. It is not as if Marino is second choice after Benton, rather he is no choice at all. Such is the extent of Benton's power and hold throughout the three novels that Marino cannot compete with either his ghost or his memory. With or without Benton, Marino is simply too flawed a character to have any chance of winning Scarpetta's affections; when the two are compared there simply is no competition.

The other contender for position of Gothic hero is of course Lucy, Scarpetta's brilliant but also desperately and deeply flawed niece. From her first appearance aged 10 in *Postmortem*, Lucy's role throughout the series is complicated as she seems to be perpetually poised between childhood and adulthood, never quite managing to move successfully from one into the other and in a constant state of turmoil and internal flux as a result of this. Consequently the way in which she as a character has been received throughout the series, and her role throughout it is frequently misunderstood:

Scarpetta's niece Lucy plays a rather conventional but important Gothic role throughout the series: she is the child who is at risk of being subsumed into evil. Thus, her affair with Carrie Grethen, the recurring villain's sidekick, differs surprisingly little from Jonathan Harker's wife giving herself up to Dracula in Bram Stoker's Gothic masterpiece. At heart, the Gothic tradition is about the dangers inherent in the transition from innocence to experience, from childhood to adulthood. And in this sense, Lucy--as tiresome as her tirades may seem to some readers--is central to the Gothic themes that run through the Scarpetta series.[196]

In a number of different ways this assessment of Lucy's character is a pertinent one, as Lucy *is* often at the cusp of evil. She is the veritable Luke Skywalker of crime fiction who is seemingly always in danger of being consumed by the dark side. The journey between innocence and experience that Lucy treads is indeed a complicated one, and there is undoubtedly confusion generated as these two conflicting states exist within Lucy simultaneously and she becomes neither one nor the other, neither innocent nor experienced. This confusion manifests itself within Lucy's often wayward behaviour, seeming irresponsibility and apparent recklessness. But whilst the transition from innocence to experience is essentially Gothic, the passage from innocence to experience is not always a voluntary one, as the statement implies, and also it is a movement usually reserved for the *heroine* of the text, and not the would-be hero. Traditionally in the Gothic this transition is of a sexual nature and is characterised by the relentless persecution of the heroine by the villain. Even by the broadest thinking possible and the most lateral interpretation of themes, in Lucy's capacity as would-be hero, her journey from innocence to experience cannot be governed by Gothic convention.

Perhaps it would be more appropriate to assess Lucy's transition within the boundaries of Gothic Romanticism rather than simply within the Gothic. In this respect Lucy shares many of the character traits of the wronged female protagonist in Gothic romances in that there is as much of the relentless (but not necessarily *conscious*) self-destruction about her. This is evident in the narrator of Daphne du Maurier's *Rebecca* and likewise there is as much rage and frustration inside her as there is in Anne Rice's child-vampire, Claudia. Despite being very different books, what links these classic Gothic romances to Lucy's role in *Black Notice*, is that the central female character in each is by no means a traditional Gothic *heroine*. Regardless of the fact that at the end of *Rebecca* the narrator does effectively 'win' Max de Winter and remain married to him, her integrity is very much compromised by the secret that she keeps for him, and the extent to which she functions as his equal more than simply a companion is indeed equivocal. Claudia, too, demonstrates similar limited success, although she does manage to secure Madeleine as a mother figure, their happiness is short lived at the vengeful hands of the Theatre Vampires.

What ties these characters together and essentially defines the role of 'heroine' within Gothic *romance* is that they are both nothing more than children thrust into the world of adulthood before they are ready and consequently their requisite transitions are not governed simply by developing sexual maturity as it is in the Gothic. It is more to do with amassing life experience in general with sexuality only a small part of this. Lucy, with her anger and frustration against the world, is a shining example of this; her constant need to prove herself, love of guns, cars and helicopters and her lack of control is essentially indicative of an existential ambiguity within Lucy – she is a mixed-up child in a very beautiful woman's body, and her resulting volatility absolutely prevents her from becoming Scarpetta's ultimate hero.

Her desperate and tragic need to have both respect and love from Scarpetta is highlighted as she struggles to tell her Aunt of the part that she played in Rocco's death: *'Please forgive me, Aunt Kay. Please say it's all right. Please don't lose your respect for me and think I've become one of them.'*[197] That she possesses such a volatile mix of emotions in something that she is acutely aware of: 'Yes, I am a Fury...I am the avenger. I admit it'[198] and that she appears to be so fixed upon a path of self-destruction is something that both Talley and Jaime Berger cannot help but notice. In *Black Notice* Talley states to Scarpetta that Lucy 'has to be Icarus and fly too close to the sun because of you. I hope she doesn't push that myth too far and fall from the sky.'[199] Berger's words too are similarly pessimistic:

If it is true that people begin to die the day they are born, then Lucy seems an exception. She is an exception to all things human, it often seems to Berger, and for this reason alone, she fears that Lucy will not live long. She envisions her compelling young face and striking body on top of a stainless-steel autopsy table, a bullet through her brain, and no matter how she struggles to strike that image from her imagination, she can't.[200]

This degree of sentimentality is arguably more romantic in feeling than it is traditionally Gothic, and this capacity for romanticism is something that Cornwell exploits in the images of Paris that she describes as she permits

Scarpetta to navigate the city's streets. Certainly by offering Europe, Paris specifically, as a location within the text Cornwell is very much painting by numbers when it comes to producing mimicry of a Gothic text, and her portrayal of the city and the Gothic influences that she uses to produce that effect are predictable, but striking nonetheless.

European Influence and the Picture of Paris

It is of course the arrival of Thomas Chandonne's decomposed body in the cargo container that docked at Richmond Port that first begins the link between Paris and America within the novel. The resulting trip to Paris taken by Scarpetta and Marino allows Cornwell to fully exploit this traditional European Gothic setting and indulge Gothic tradition by giving us a description so saturated with atmosphere and Gothic symbolism that it becomes strongly reminiscent of early Gothic writing:

> I walked around, feeling the damp cold of old stone and air blowing off
> the river as I moved around in the darkness of deep shadows…A faint
> breeze stirred acacia trees and touched my skin as I replayed what Dr.
> Stvan had said about the man who had come to her door.[201]

Indeed it is very hard to read Cornwell's description of Paris with its cobbled streets, dark alleyways and seventeenth-century dwellings without being reminded of earlier work by Victor Hugo, Edgar Allan Poe, Gaston Leroux and even the much more contemporary Anne Rice. Certainly as far as Hugo, Leroux and Rice are concerned each of *their* texts feature within them a creature or creatures outcast from society and forced to live underground, foraging existence for themselves only under the cover of darkness, and this is of course exactly how Chandonne lives too.

If just setting the novel in Paris was not enough, Cornwell ensures that we cannot miss the Gothic tone of the text by permitting Scarpetta to view the Paris Opera House from her hotel room window, and one is forced to wonder if the view of the 'gilt sculptures on the old opera house across the street' that flaunt 'their golden, naked beauty before the gods'[202] is the same view that greeted opera goers back in 1909 when Leroux was first publishing in the French newspaper *Le Gaulois*, *his* serial story about a disfigured genius forced to live within the cellars and vaults of the theatre. Whilst it is true to say that Cornwell's depiction of Paris is deeply rooted in traditional Gothic, there is more than just writer's fancy in her descriptions. Certainly by seeming to follow in the path of Gothic whimsy in this fashion Cornwell is managing intentionally to pitch the moody ambience of Paris against the rationale and reasoning influence of America.

This should not be misconstrued however, to assume that Cornwell is portraying Paris in a negative light, or that she is making judgments that are detrimental to the city in any way. Rather it seems that through her Gothic depiction Cornwell is able to realise for the reader the romantic ambience of the city, and indeed it is revealed to us during Scarpetta's stay in Paris that she once visited the city on a romantic break with Benton. That Chandonne should be able to practise his psychopathic behaviour and sexual degradation of his victims in a city so revered for its romance is nothing short of horrific, and made more abhorrent as a result of Cornwell's careful depiction of the city.

Despite having such strong French connections however, it is only during this brief spell in *Black Notice* that the action leaves the US; the remainder of the text and those that follow are located back in America (with the exception of a very short trip to Poland by Lucy and Rudy). The fact that so much of the narrative is removed from its European Gothic roots does not however limit the potential for *Black Notice*, or indeed the two texts that follow it, to be considered as Gothic texts. Indeed Cornwell uses more than simply setting and character type to give her novels Gothic 'substance'; and one of the other ways she does this is with regard to the narrative structure that she adopts in her writing, particularly the 'confessional' tone that is evident in *The Last Precinct*, the second novel of the trilogy.

Confession and the Gothic: The Role of Anna Zenner

Although epistolary novels have been around for centuries (the earliest recorded example of a novel of this form is Aphra Behn's 1684 *Love-Letters Between a Nobleman and His Sister*) it was not until Mary Shelley wrote *Frankenstein* that the form began to appear within Gothic writing. Because of the confessional and insightful tone that the form afforded, it found a willing host within the Gothic novel, and writers of the genre were able to use the first person perspective as a means of generating credibility and instilling terror into its readers. Perhaps the most famous Gothic novel to adopt the epistolary form is Stoker's *Dracula*, and the novel benefits significantly from it in a number of ways. Because essentially the epistolary novel deals with letters and diary entries it is one of the few genres that demands prose to be written for the most part in first person narrative. First person narrative is important because it permits the reader to actually get inside the mind of the character and expose a range of emotions that otherwise simply could not be recorded.

Written in the first person, *The Last Precinct* opens in the immediate aftermath of Chandonne's attempted attack upon Scarpetta, and as it progresses the role that she holds as Gothic heroine is compounded even further; her professional position becomes more precarious and her personal resolve more unstable. She finds herself under investigation by a special grand jury for the murder of Diane Bray, narrowly escapes being murdered by Jay Talley (who by this point has been identified as being the brother of the deformed Chandonne), is ultimately homeless, and has her professional reputation on the verge of ruin. Certainly her predicament is understood by Jaime Berger who warns her of Chandonne's ultimate intention: 'He has started a deadly, cruel process, the violation of Kay Scarpetta.'[203]

In desiring to continue the Gothic theme, although perhaps with a little more subtlety, Cornwell uses *this* novel's entirely American setting to engage with a more American form of the Gothic genre, that which was identified in Chapter 2 as being significantly *less* sensational or explicit and altogether *more* to do with psychology and manifestations of guilt and sorrow. In a very modern and altogether new take upon the epistolary form that appeared in earlier Gothic texts such as *Frankenstein* and *Dracula*, Cornwell uses the firelight sessions that take place between Scarpetta and Zenner as a credible means of extracting confession and insight from Scarpetta and to this effect where once the soul may have been bared through the *written* medium of letter or diary entry, in *this* text it is all about *spoken* thoughts and feelings as Zenner attempts to counsel her friend through the atrocities that have befallen her.

It is a process that Scarpetta finds difficult, readily admitting that she chooses not to 'acknowledge' that part of her brain that permits her to think reflectively and to process her emotions; she even goes so far as to label this part of her as 'useless'[204]. Despite the fact that talking in this fashion, confessing and admitting to her weaknesses as she perceives them is difficult for her, it is nevertheless a necessary part of her undoing if we are to truly comprehend the way in which Scarpetta is being portrayed as the ultimate Gothic heroine. In *Black Notice* we were made aware of her physical vulnerabilities and now in *The Last Precinct* we are becoming aware of her psychological vulnerability too. Having said this however, it must be pointed out that Cornwell has not laid Scarpetta open for our voyeuristic pleasure and we are not supposed to take any sort of enjoyment from seeing her exposed in this fashion. It is a rite of passage that she must go through in order to prove to herself that she has enough mettle to survive the investigation by the special grand jury and the trial that she finds herself on. In this respect Scarpetta, like Stoker's heroine Mina Harker, in the absence of anyone else to do it for her, assumes responsibility for herself, and effectively becomes her own hero.

Certainly by the time *Blow Fly* begins much of the success that Scarpetta has experienced at the end of *The Last Precinct* is maintained and she has managed to claw back some semblance of normality, but the events of the previous two novels have clearly taken their toll, she carries with her an air of 'weariness, a sadness as immutable as the stumps and knees of cypress trees in the swamps and bayous of her [Robillard's] Louisiana home.'[205] She is uninterested in her food and uninterested in life. To all extents and purposes she has hit a stumbling block. Confessing that she is unable to 'get over Benton Wesley'[206], Cornwell details Scarpetta's present existence to such an extent that the reader is left in absolutely no doubt whatsoever as to the depths into which Scarpetta has fallen:

> Life was good. Then it wasn't and never would be again. So much went wrong. So much was spoiled and lost and could never be restored.
> Three years ago, she was well along her journey to disaster…The pre-crash Scarpetta was impeccably, if not rigidly, intellectual, completely confident of her knowledge, her truthfulness and her ability to excavate for answers. She was a legend in law enforcement and criminal justice…
> Now she has no staff except her secretary, Rose, who followed her to Florida with the excuse that it would be nice to "retire" near West Palm Beach.[207]

Blow Fly is of course different to its predecessor in that within the text the narrative once again returns to the third person and because of this we can rightly assume that this novel will not be quite as probing nor will it focus so exclusively upon Scarpetta herself. In fact to ensure that we as reader realise just how different a novel this one will be compared with its predecessor, Cornwell ensures that the novel opens in what is arguably a more brutal and explicit example of modern crime fiction, and that is with the offender, Jean-Paul Chandonne (aka Jay Talley) poised above his latest victim. Written in the present tense, the novel takes on a greater sense of urgency than was present in either *Black Notice* or *The Last Precinct* and there is from the outset of the text the feeling that within this last installment of the Chandonne saga fever pitch will be reached and some form of final showdown will take place.

In continuing the Gothic theme of hounded heroine the Scarpetta that we meet in the beginning of the novel is a character wearied and without sufficient focus and direction to avoid becoming an easy target from the villains within the text. Overwhelmed by the company of her students in the restaurant she confesses to herself that the situation is 'out of her control'[208] and in a very un-Scarpetta like acknowledgment of defeat, merely sits back and 'surrenders'[209]. With her eye off the ball so to speak, Scarpetta becomes a pawn within the novel, easy to manipulate and consequently finds herself unwittingly thrust into the middle of a game that has been carefully orchestrated by Benton. The game however, backfires spectacularly and Scarpetta finds herself threatened once again by Jean-Baptiste Chandonne, and at the end of the novel believes that she is about to come face to face with him once more. It is a somewhat melodramatic plot line to say the least, and the course of the three novels detail more attacks upon Scarpetta, of varying degrees and effects, than frankly should be credible. However, insofar as examining the ways in which the novels adopt traditional Gothic motif then clearly Cornwell's prose style becomes more plausible. After all, the everyday and the norm have never been sustainable fodder for the Gothic, and these three novels are no exception to this rule.

Far-fetched as some of the themes may be, they are certainly not without purpose, and that purpose is the carefully and deliberately timed re-introduction of Benton Wesley to not only this particular novel (*Blow Fly*), but also his return to the series as a whole. His timing could not be more precise as he returns at the point at which Scarpetta, in defence of Albert Dard, prepares to face what she believes to be her tormentor on the stairs of the Dard plantation house. Specifically being in this location not only emphasises Scarpetta's vulnerability, but also places her at the heart of that which is critical to modern crime fiction, the 'gothicized, fearsome and paranoid world of lecherous and brutal men who...threaten not only her physical safety but her psychic equilibrium as well.'[210] It is a situation that Scarpetta must face head on and successfully navigate her way through if she is to fully realise her role as heroine and have her reward for doing so, the reward which is of course the return of Benton Wesley.

That he returns at this point (with more than just a whiff of a fairytale ending about it) is crucial to our perception of Benton as ultimate hero. Undoubtedly had he not been there, Scarpetta would have been in mortal danger. The Dard household with its many links to the Chandonne cartel is simply not a safe place for her to be. In returning when he does he is able to save her from the total destruction that threatens her. His reappearance is not just about realising his role as hero however, it is also much to do with realising Scarpetta's achievements throughout the previous two texts. Yes, he has come to save her, but she has *earned* that right to be saved (as ultimately all Gothic heroines have to do) by the show of guts and determination in previous novels and in doing this Cornwell is absolutely adhering to one of the strictest rules of earliest Gothic writing, that the heroine, showing enough reserve and mettle should be rewarded in the manner that befits her. As Benton himself states, part of her transition from victim to heroine was to 'confront him [Chandonne] before he died.'[211]

Up until this point Benton as a character has largely been ignored, simply because he has not been a physical presence in the text. Of course the letter that he wrote to her at the beginning of *Black Notice* resulted in a sort of spiritual presence for Scarpetta and this protective arm extended to varying degrees across the three texts, but ultimately as a protective influence in Scarpetta's life he has been gone. As a result of this anything that we learn about Benton within these texts comes from people talking about him and consequently we have only been able to gather insight into his character through what other people think of him. So what impressions *do* we form of this character then, this renowned FBI profiler, through other people's assessments of him? Interestingly they are not all as positive as one might assume. During one of her confessional sessions with Anna Zenner, Scarpetta reveals that their relationship was troubled at the time of his murder, admitting that she and Benton had lost their intimacy, and that the sexual aspect to their relationship had become 'an abandoned airport that looked normal from a distance but had no-one in the tower.'[212]

When probed further it is revealed that there were a number of things that she and Benton never shared with each other, and Scarpetta admits that 'there were deep places in me he never reached. I also never wanted him to, didn't want to get that intense, that close.'[213] In fact through her discussions with Zenner, Scarpetta reveals a number of incidents that suggest that for whatever reason Benton did not posses the requisite tenderness and affection that one would expect from a potential traditional Gothic hero. Coupled with this is Scarpetta's sister Dorothy's assessment of Benton as 'weak' and of having 'not enough sap' in the 'tree' or enough 'yolk' in the 'egg'[214], the result of which is that our belief in Benton as a knight in shining armour begins to waver a little. Of course for Benton to be completely perfect would perhaps be a little too fairytale, a little too clichéd, and so what we have in Benton is a hero cast in the same mould as Will Graham of *Silence of the Lambs* and John Rebus of Rankin's texts, and that is a hero who is flawed: not perfect but good enough.

Representations of America

Earlier in this chapter reference was made to the seeming representation of America as rational and the way in which this appears to contrast with the passion and romanticism with which Paris is associated. This contrast is particularly evident in *Black Notice* and in *The Last Precinct*, specifically the romantic memories that Scarpetta has of her time with Benton in Paris and the manner in which these memories are tarnished by the sheer awfulness of what Jean-Baptiste has done to the women of Paris. But there is a similar degree of social commentary offered within *Blow Fly* also, and this is directly to do with the apparently exclusively American propensity for violence. For the most part this theme relates to Scarpetta's blatant assessment that there is a 'not so far-fetched notion that America's karma, sadly, seems to be for us to kill each other'[215] and indeed there are a number of ways in which this seeming preoccupation for society to turn against itself and become so self-destructive manifests itself within the text. During his videotaped interview with Jaime Berger, Chandonne himself makes reference to his belief that 'Americans kill people even when they are innocent' and that this 'fact' 'is well known.'[216] By using the Jamestown setting Cornwell is able to explore this concept further, detailing that Jamestown itself is the location for what is widely believed to be the first murder on American soil; the shooting of an unknown and unidentified man in 1607. Certainly by including this detail in her writing Cornwell does seem to be forcing her readers to ask themselves if, in light of what they are reading, so very much has changed at all since then.

Chandonne's claim that he has been set up by the American FBI, CIA and Interpol and effectively framed for murders he did not commit is an interesting reference to the perceived notions of spying and tracking that these institutions have been associated with in the past and are widely perceived to still be doing today. Within the context of understanding American history and the degree of 'spying' carried out by institutions such as these in the Cold War years, even Scarpetta acknowledges that 'maybe Chandonne was offering a hint of truth when he persisted in his seemingly absurd claim that he is the victim of some huge political conspiracy.'[217] Whilst Chandonne's beliefs are completely fabricated and nothing more than an attempt to make himself appear innocent of any wrongdoing, the notion of conspiracy is not lost on Scarpetta who herself has been subjected to a hateful conspiracy masterminded by Diane Bray, the ultimate purpose of which was to sabotage Scarpetta's career irrecoverably from the inside by actions committed by Chuck Ruffin.

There is a great amount of paranoia and suspicion, not all of it unfounded, evident within this text. Resultingly the novel deals with many of the themes central to the other American novels that have been examined hereto in this book, and in as much as Cornwell brings to the genre that is *new*, it is the same old notions of suspicion at work that formed such an important part of the work of both Bloch and Harris. By the time we reach *Blow Fly*, the last text in this mini-series, the theme of paranoia is still very evident, but the focus, or the root cause of it, has altered dramatically. The first edition of the text did not appear in print until 2003, and following the events of 9/11 the world, including America, was indeed a very different place. The impact of the events of that day are glaringly apparent as Lucy comments on and criticises the very lazy attitudes to safety and security demonstrated by those that she encounters at passport control:

> Had he bothered to unzip those two duffel bags and dig through the clothing he would have discovered a tactical baton…The world is full of lazy fools like him.[218]

In *Blow Fly* it is Talley, Chandonne's evil twin brother, who takes centre stage as the villain at large, and despite the psychopathic similarities between them, in terms of their roles as Gothic villains, the two could not be more different. On the one hand we have Jean-Baptiste, a veritable celebration of Gothic excess, deformed, monstrous with more than a hint of werewolf association, and on the other is Talley, beautiful, cultured and successful. There is no mistaking the irony here: Cornwell clearly intends for us to make comparisons between the two and to ask ourselves which of these two murdering twins is the worst, the more frightening and the more dangerous. That the question is so easily answered holds great significance for interpreting Cornwell's understanding of the threats posed to American society at the beginning of the 21st century. Certainly Jean-Baptiste is dangerous – he is a killer after all, but he is no match for Talley, master manipulator and master of disguise extraordinaire. In effect Talley becomes so much more the worse of the two because that which he appears to be is so diametrically opposed to that which he is. He has had a privileged upbringing, savouring the fine wines from his father's wine cellar, enjoying a fine education and the experience of high society. His killing, although just as inexcusable as Chandonne's, is without rationale or reason, the only motivation for it provided by Benton who identifies that Talley kills because he is 'bored'[219].

Of course we cannot look to the character of Jay Talley without addressing the issues of identity that not only hold such a strong theme throughout the three texts, but also form the basis to the way in which 21st-century America is represented in the texts. By the time *Blow Fly* appeared in 2003, American suspicions were very different to those that were exposed in *Black Notice* and *The Last Precinct*. Of the three texts, arguably *Blow Fly* is the most concerned with identity and self-awareness, specifically *knowing* who our friends and colleagues really are and *believing* that they are actually who claim to be. During her time in Poland Lucy successfully takes on another persona to avoid repercussion from the murder of Rocco, and Benton is discovered to be alive and well, living his life under a specialised witness protection program as the homosexual Tom Haviland. There is also a significant shift in the degree of paranoia experienced by, and lack of focus evident among, the central characters, and this as is evident in Lucy's forgetting to remove her tactical baton from the crime scene as it is in Scarpetta's accompanying Albert Dard back to the Dard plantation. Indeed it is a change in tone and theme so dramatic that it is impossible to ignore or overlook, and to find Cornwell's rationale for making this change, we must look beyond the confines of the book and consider the factors affecting American society at the time.

Much of the tension of the novel is generated by the use of the present tense throughout; certainly it contributes to the greater degree of emphasis upon the *here and now* of the story. By writing in the present tense Cornwell can add to the degree of urgency within the text and also make her observations about social security and unease more relevant and poignant. As a result of this *Blow Fly* is almost certainly one of the first examples of modern crime fiction to present the threat of terrorism as being the new Communism, in that it has very quickly (in the wake of the September 11 attacks) become yet another faceless monster to fear. The lack of direction, terror and confusion that followed this very difficult and also very recent event in American history is very much evident in the seemingly disorganised structure of the texts as a whole. Throughout the narrative the focus shifts from Chandonne's cell, to Talley's shack, to Baton Rouge and also to wherever Benton happens to be as he anonymously tries to orchestrate proceedings to locate and apprehend Talley and also to bring about the downfall of the Chandonne cartel.

Of course just as *Black Notice* had a role to play given its status as the opening text to the series, so too does *Blow Fly* have a job to do. It is in the capacity of having to bring about closure that the novel has to act as a summary to the story and bring about a conclusion that offers satisfaction for the readers that have followed it this far. It is effectively the putting together of the last few pieces of the jigsaw, of forcing end-game, and amassing the half-weaved strands of plot and this is another reason why the structure of the text appears to be so jolty.

Despite its seeming lack of direction however, the text has three distinct purposes. The arrest of Talley and Kiffin (which does not happen – Kiffin is shot and Talley escapes) and the return of Benton not only to Scarpetta, but to America as a whole, are two of these, and the third is the clarification of the purpose of The Last Precinct itself, the renegade institute created by Lucy as an alternative to the failing institution of the FBI. Regardless of the title of the previous novel, it is not until *Blow Fly* that we can actually begin to see the significance that The Last Precinct holds in its capacity to generate results where the FBI and Interpol have failed. Despite the fact that Interpol has Rocky Caggagio flagged as a Red Notice, alerting roughly 182 different countries to the very pressing need to have him intercepted and apprehended, it ultimately falls to Lucy and Rudy to do the job themselves, and that job is to locate and to murder him as part of the first wave of attack upon the Chandonne cartel.

In permitting the somewhat lawless and unregulated Last Precinct to achieve this successfully and thus highlighting institutional failure on the part of the FBI and Interpol, Cornwell is making serious comment about the greater failing of the American government to protect its people, as she has Lucy explain:

> It's sort of turned into a secret society. There's a real buzz on the street.
> When shit hits, call The Last Precinct – where you go when there's
> nowhere left.[220]

Clearly faith in Interpol and the FBI has failed, and they quite simply are no match for this new breed of criminal that stalks the street in modern society. It is a bold advancement to make, but its sensationalism and excessiveness is made acceptable and plausible within the boundaries of the Gothic tone to the series that were set up in *Black Notice*. It adopting Gothic motif Cornwell has very much continued in the tradition of using the form (to varying degrees) to exploit cultural fear and unease, and it will be interesting to see in the next chapter to what extent British writer Mo Hayder manages to do this in *her* examples of Gothic-influenced writing that reject traditional European and American settings in favour of an altogether new breed of modern crime fiction.

CHAPTER SEVEN

Abandoning the Gothic's European Roots: A Journey into the Unknown in Mo Hayder's *Tokyo*, *Ritual* and *Pig Island*

I T is no misplaced perception that much modern crime fiction is written by either British or American writers and set in either British or American locations. Such is the nature of the genre that plausibility and credibility are so important to the texts that writers rarely stray away from areas in which they feel comfortable, whether this be in relation to setting (Ian Rankin writing about his native Scotland for example) or the particulars of law enforcement and legal technicalities with which they are familiar (Patricia Cornwell actually worked at the Virginia Medical Examiner's Office for a number of years). There is of course a great deal of logic behind this, and it must be incredibly difficult to write effectively about parts of the world or issues of policing in areas with which you are unfamiliar. Nevertheless there has been in recent years a small, but significant number of authors who have begun to move away from the more usual settings outlined above, taken their texts further afield and begun to question crime and the way in which it is perceived and understood in other countries and cultures.

One of the most successful authors to do this in recent years is British writer, Mo Hayder. Whilst it is true that Hayder's Jack Caffery series for the most part tends to stay within many of the boundaries of conventional modern crime fiction, her book *Ritual* and the stand alone novels *Tokyo* and *Pig Island* are very atypical in terms of the crimes and cultural influences that they explore. The way in which Hayder manages to carve out yet another new direction for the genre, and the extent to which she is successful in doing this, will be the main focus of this chapter.

Eastern Influence: Representations of Culture

Published in Britain in 2004, *Tokyo* (in America the novel did not appear until 2005, and then under the title *The Devil of Nanking*) is Hayder's first novel not to feature her successful DI, Jack Caffery. Instead it features no alternative law enforcement officer at all and becomes part of the small-sub genre of modern crime fiction that has an amateur sleuth at its core. The novel focuses on the search for answers in relation to a particular event that happened during the Japanese invasion and massacre of Nanking in 1937. The 'search' is carried out by a young English woman named Grey Hutchins who has travelled to Tokyo to seek out filmed evidence relating to this specific event that has completely taken over and shaped her life so dramatically. The footage is held by a Chinese professor, Shi Chongming, who agrees to show her the film only if she manages to obtain the mysterious elixir that is in the possession of one of Japan's most feared yakuzas, Junzo Fuyuki.

The novel itself is carefully and deliberately structured, and moves between the present in the form of Grey's experiences in Tokyo, and the horrific events surrounding the fall of Nanking in 1937 that have been recorded in brutal honesty in Shi Chongming's diary. Continuing the trend in modern crime fiction not to shy away from reality and to confront issues explicitly, Hayder's revelations do not always make for comfortable reading and Chongming's diary is deeply unsettling in its depiction of the atrocities carried out by the Japanese soldiers. The novel is Gothic, or demonstrates Gothic influence, in a number of different ways, and these will be explored briefly before beginning to look at the very many *new* things that Hayder offers to the genre.

Like many early Gothic texts the novel is mostly to do with the relentless pursuit of that which remains unattainable and the descent into obsession that this pursuit causes. In her desperate need to have her questions answered and discover proof that the event that she read about did actually take place, Grey travels to Tokyo with the sole purpose of tracking down Shi Chongming and confronting him as to the videotape's whereabouts. Unbeknownst to Grey, Chongming too has come to Tokyo in order that he may track down Fuyuki and lay to rest the demons of *his* past. That these two characters are so relentlessly dogged by the events of their pasts is a very deliberate manipulation of early Gothic motif. Certainly the novel presses upon its readers the idea that the past is an inescapable presence within each of us, and that at some point our pasts will catch up with us, no matter to what extent we try to suppress them.

Despite the physical and cultural distances from more traditional Western locations that Tokyo offers, Hayder is keen to apply many of the techniques of personification of place that were such a strong part of early Gothic writing. Tokyo is presented as a city that by all accounts lives and breathes in much the same way as those that inhabit it do. It has a life of its own and a history that tells as much of a story as those that people it do:

> ...a warren of cranky little streets jammed into the crevices behind
> the skyscrapers, a dark, breathing patch like a jungle floor...Crooked
> houses leaned wearily against each other, rotten and broken – exhausted
> survivors of decades of earthquakes, fires, bombing. In the cracks
> between the houses lush, carnivorous-looking plants crowded together.[221]

In Grey's initial assessment of the city there is much to remind us of the way in which Edinburgh was revealed to us in many of the Rankin texts; that behind the front of the city there lurks another side to the metropolis, and that this city centre too has seen its fair share of hardship and trouble. Indeed it is through Grey's navigation of the city that its real underworld, the shady and dark presence of the yakuza, is revealed to us. Behind the bright lights of the city, the intellectual prowess of its universities and the very public way in which people remember and respect their dead, there is a terrible secret waiting to be uncovered. Alone and uncertain, Grey is taken under the 'protective' wing of the mysterious Jason, a dangerous and altogether new breed of Gothic villain who thrives on Grey's vulnerability and makes it his mission to possess her not only sexually, but through uncovering the secret that she is keeping.

Offered a room in his house, an equally mysterious and dangerous place, Grey finds herself residing within a rambling and dilapidated old building reminiscent of early Gothic abodes. Complete with sealed-off areas, overgrown gardens, submerged cellars and wings that are literally falling apart, the house ceases to become merely just a place to live and becomes a complex representation of the mindset and psychological abnormalities of not only Jason, but of Grey too. However, despite his twisted nature, it is not Jason who becomes the ultimate villain in the text. This role is reserved for Junzo Fuyuki, a seemingly benign wheelchair-bound old man who led a very active and destructive role in the Nanking invasion and now surrounds himself with the most psychopathic and dangerous villains that Japan has to offer.

Junzo Fuyuki and the Quest for Immortality

Fuyuki himself is, like so many earlier Gothic villains, consumed with the desire to *live*. Through his reliance upon, and his unwavering belief that it is the special properties of his 'medicine' that keep him alive, Hayder is offering us a very modern twist upon the old Gothic theme of ensuring immortality through ancestral lineage; Fuyuki is not interested in producing heirs to continue in his name – he wants to continue to experience life for himself and his desire to achieve this knows no boundaries. He is powerful and dangerous and his potential for atrocity is a very tangible presence within the novel. Certainly this air of danger is felt by his associate Bison as he realizes the grave mistake that he has made in mocking the 'potent' power of Fuyuki's draft. Shocked and shamed into silence Bison spends the rest of the evening in silence, eerily preoccupied by the foreboding presence of Fuyuki's nurse, as we are told he keeps 'glancing across at the ominous shadow of the Nurse. His cheeks were damp, his eyes watered and for the rest of the night his Adam's apple worked painfully as if he might be sick.'[222]

Indeed Fuyuki is no ordinary villain, and Bison is right to fear him. Within the novel Hayder has granted this mysterious character huge status as a modern Gothic monster. With cannibalistic and vampiristic connotations aplenty he is the ultimate consumer; a creature of entitlement who believes that he can have whatever he wants by the sheer force of fear and intimidation. Like many of his villainous predecessors he is ruthless and arrogant. He is a fighter and will fight his corner, and protect his secret at all costs. He is a beast without morals and very much a man to be feared.

The Role of the Past: Causal Dependency

It has already been mentioned, albeit briefly, that within the narrative there is much emphasis upon the ongoing influence of the past, and there is a great deal more to say about it still, specifically the way in which Hayder credits the past as being a fundamental part of identity and critical in understanding why we come to be where we are. At its most basic level the past and the present are shown to be linked in the way that in which the novel is structured, with Shi Chongming occupying roles in the present and also in the past through the re-reading of the diary that he kept in 1937. The link between these two worlds is Grey herself and her presence forces Chongming to face that part of his personal history that he has tried to keep secret. Grey also has a past within the novel waiting to be uncovered and that relates to the trauma surrounding her teenage pregnancy and the loss of her own baby.

The joining of two different worlds (be they the past and the present or the public and the private) is reminiscent of the way in which Mary Crane served to represent the joining of two worlds in Robert Bloch's *Psycho*. It is similar to the way in which Jonathan Harker provided a link between the very different worlds of England and Transylvania in *Dracula* and also of the way in which Elizabeth caused conflict between the scientific yearnings of Victor Frankenstein and his need for domesticity. In looking at the bigger picture in this way it is indeed possible to draw comparisons between the texts and it can be more easily seen that from the outset much of the tension of the Gothic is to do with the collision of ideals when contrasting and conflicting modes of behaviour (whether this be old versus new ideals, public versus private identities or Eastern and Western cultures) are forced to meet.

Despite the past being often such a destructive influence upon the present, the exposure of secrets and their links to the past are a fundamental part of the Gothic and the nature of the genre guarantees that if there is a secret to find, no matter how hard someone has tried to bury it, it *will* come to light at some point in the duration of the novel.

In revealing the secrets of the past authors of modern crime fiction, in particular authors of recent modern crime fiction are exploring the concept that the past is intrinsically related to identity, either personal or cultural, and that it holds a key role in defining who we are. That we all have such a deep-rooted connection to our past is one of the most significant theories behind the concept of and psychological application of causal dependency.

At its most basic interpretation, causality refers to the relationship between cause and effect. It recognises that every effect or outcome has a cause (or reason) behind it, and that to understand the effect you firstly need to examine the cause. It is a philosophy that dates back to Aristotle and continues to be a topic in modern philosophical discussion. Within *this* particular text the relationship between Nanking (the cause) and both Grey and Chongming's predicaments (the effect) is easy to understand and to interpret, and consequently Chongming's presence in Tokyo can be seen to be a direct result of those events that took place in China in 1937. Grey's presence in the city is also entirely linked to events of her personal past, and this relationship is made explicit by the structure of the novel and the link between the past and the present that the structure permits.

The novel also questions evil and the extent to which we are capable of evil if we remain ignorant of the full extent of our wrongdoing. Like much other modern crime fiction, *Tokyo* is concerned as much about the actual crimes that have been committed, as the aftermath of the crime upon those that have survived it. The aftermath was a subject matter very rarely addressed in early Gothic fiction and these earliest novels were prone to detailing a happy ending upon which the novel concluded. Certainly *The Castle of Otranto* is an excellent example of this tendency within the Gothic to advocate peace and harmony at the end of the text as we are given no insight as to how Isabella fared in the weeks immediately after being chased through the castle by the psychopathic and crazed Manfred. Likewise in the earliest form of detective fiction there is little reference to the way in which those affected by the crime managed afterwards, and it is only in the advent of modern crime fiction that authors have begun really to pay attention and to explore the ramifications of crime upon both people and their societies.

Consequently there is scope within *Tokyo* to understand the novel as detailing the journeys taken by Grey and Chongming as they attempt to overcome the traumas of their past and the manner in which they begin to heal themselves. The novel is much to do with transition, as both Grey and Chongming move from states of ignorance into states of awareness whereby they gain the knowledge that they seek. Whilst we understand that transition, specifically the growth from innocence to experience is a traditional Gothic theme, the way in which Hayder treats the theme is very different in *Tokyo*. First and foremost is the absence of a sexual aspect to the transitions. Although Grey is pursued sexually by Jason, his pursuit of her is not a part of that which she has come to Tokyo for and any sexual relationship that she has with him is consensual. Whereas typically in the Gothic transition was a process for the most part *forced* upon the heroine, both Grey and Chongming take it upon *themselves* to seek the answers the need in order to find the peace of mind that eludes them.

Hayder also follows traditional Gothic form by ensuring that by the point at which the novel ends most of the villains within the text have been suitably punished; Jason is killed and Fuyuki dies in his sleep. The only other villain not accounted for is of course the nurse, Ogawa, and one feels that it is neither in Hayder's nature, or indeed her writing style to offer her readers absolute peace of mind by offering a complete case-closed ending to her text. For Grey and Chongming the ending of the text is, to a degree, a more positive process. Grey finds the answer that she has been seeking for almost ten years and Chongming is finally able to release his video-tape and begin the process of identifying and punishing those who were guilty of the most unspeakable and horrific of crimes. Whilst it would be too great a leap to take to say that within the text the guilty are punished and the innocent rewarded, it is perhaps true that the particular evil within the novel is largely eradicated. It would certainly be a step too far to define both Grey and Chongming as innocent; the best that can be said for them is that they acted blindly, and most importantly that whatever happened, what they did not do was to *intend* to hurt anybody. There seems to be a clear meaning here about the nature of innocence in modern society and the extent to which to some degree we are all guilty of something, and the best we can hope for is that whatever wrong was done it was not done out of evil.

Whilst the way in which Hayder has manipulated some traditional Gothic motifs and yet stayed more true to others in *Tokyo* is interesting, it is her choice of setting that is the most interesting part of studying this new breed of Gothic tale. In choosing a culture so alien to most Western audiences, Hayder is indeed playing with the boundaries of the genre in a way that quite simply has not been done before and it is interesting that despite her alternative location the fundaments of the genre remain unchanged. It appears that in Hayder's world man's capacity for evil is just as horrific, and yet just as plausible, regardless of location or setting. Depravity, it seems, is not exclusively an American or a British phenomenon, but a worldwide one.

A Clash of Culture in *Ritual*

Although located in England, Bristol to be exact, Hayder's 2008 novel *Ritual* is also greatly focused on a non-British culture, that of West African superstition. Whereas in *Tokyo* it was Grey who travelled to Japan and so the novel was able to be seen through the eyes of a Westerner in a foreign land, in *Ritual* the cultural clash occurs on British soil. The novel centres upon the grisly find of a human hand in Bristol harbour and the police investigation that follows the find. *Ritual*, like *Tokyo* is a complex novel and there are a great many different strands to the story that all operate concurrently; as a consequence the study of the text in this chapter will extend only so far as to what is relevant to our understanding of the ways in which this novel can be seen to be using Gothic influence within the narrative.

Within such a complex novel it is indeed difficult to know where to begin. There is so much going on at once – so many interlinked strands – that the narrative is simultaneously more than one person's story and each aspect is cleverly interwoven to make the transition between plots seamless.

Essentially the detective aspect to the novel is combined of DI Jack Caffery and Sergeant Flea Marley who team up to try and find out who is responsible for the placing of the hands within the harbour. Although Bristol is at first assessment not one of the more obvious locations in which to set a Gothic text, it is not without relevance within the context of the novel. Bristol itself has historical significance in terms of the position it once held as a key operator within the transatlantic slave trade; the city was in possession of many slave ships that as soon as they emptied themselves of the manufactured cargo they took to the African shores, would fill up again with African slaves and ship them on to the Caribbean Islands before returning to Britain. Whilst there is no actual slavery as such within the novel, there is an alternative form of slavery at work within the narrative, and that is the way in which so many of the characters appear not to be able to operate under their own free will. Caffery and Marley are slaves to their pasts, deeply affected by the mystery that still surrounds the disappearances of their family members, brother and parents respectively, Mossy is a drug addict – his movements always controlled by trying to score his next hit. Skinny is equally enslaved by Tig, and must carry out the orders that he is given.

In providing the reader with such extensive information about the background of her characters, Hayder is continuing the trend for modern crime fiction to be as much about the issues affecting the detectives as it is about the crime and criminals that it portrays. The disappearance of Caffery's brother has been a continuing theme within each of the other novels to feature the detective, and despite his relocation to Bristol it still affects him very much, continuing to affect the way in which he carries out his job and interacts with the people that he meets. Marley is similarly haunted by the disappearance of her parents, the victims of a failed dive that took place at Bushman's Hole, a diving hole in the middle of the Kalahari Desert. Through the course of the novel we are given insight into the way in which Marley is still coming to terms with the manner in which her parents disappeared, and this insight manifests itself through the interaction that she has with Kaiser and her desperation to understand the 'message' from her mother that she experienced during a drug-induced hallucination.

In the same way that *Tokyo* juxtaposed Eastern and Western culture, in *Ritual* there is a similar linking between Western and African cultures. In novels that are 'seen through' Western eyes as such, much of the meaning of the text is relatable to the way in which Westerners respond to and attempt to understand the customs and traditions of those cultures that remain alien to us. The discovery of the hands leads Caffery and Marley to the identification of an African tradition that is being carried out within Bristol and that is the use of severed human hands to bring about success in business. Just as she did in *Tokyo*, Hayder refuses to shy away from the brutality of the crime and the explicit detail in which the crime is carried out. In *Tokyo* we were able to witness firsthand the shocking murder of Chongming's wife and the theft of their baby through the film of the event that Grey watches; in *Ritual* too we are granted similar proximity to the crime – the removal of Mossy's hands as the novel carefully moves between past and present in a manner that allows us to actually witness the crime taking place.

This in itself is a new feature of modern crime fiction and denotes a definite change in the direction in which the author wishes to take the reader. Not content to let us hear of or about the crime through the eyes of the detective, forensic team or pathologist, Hayder has deliberately crafted and structured her novels so that we are presented with brutal reality of what has happened. In previous examples discussed hereto the description of the crime scenes has often been graphic; and the detailing of the murder of Diane Bray in *Black Notice* is an excellent example of this. But because we are only taken to the crime scene *after* the event has taken place a large part of the horror has been removed and there is still an element of detachment for the reader, a small modicum of comfort to be taken from the fact that we did not bear witness to the attack as it actually took place. There is no such degree of comfort to be taken from Hayder's work as she rejects absolutely the 'babysitting' approach that generates such distance between the reader and the very real brutality of the crimes.

In interview Hayder readily confesses that the graphic nature that characterises so much of her writing is a deliberate movement, engineered at creating a form of honesty and trust between herself and her readers, and she states that:

> In most crime novels the violent act, usually the murder, is the engine.
> Take that away and there is little left to drive the story along. So I do
> get a little cross with authors who aren't precise about the violence
> they're using to create tension because I feel they're being dishonest with
> their readers. If people don't like the blood and violence in my books,
> fine, they can always close the cover and put it aside and maybe read a
> romance instead.[223]

Certainly it is true that the detailing of the crime, the removal of Mossy's hands in this example, makes for shocking reading and one of the ways that

Hayder manages to achieve greater proximity to Mossy is by shifting to the present tense. The aftermath of the crime, also in the present tense, is equally if not more so horrific:

> Mossy lies on his back, tears running down his face…It's the first time in what seems like a lifetime that the pain has gone down to a level where he can concentrate, to think about his situation. He's no idea how long it's been since Uncle took his hands…And it is this he keeps coming back to. *They are my fucking hands…Give me back my fucking hands, you cunts…* Now he's thinking straight he knows the truth. There's no going back. He's going to die here.[224]

Whilst *Ritual* is perhaps the least Gothic of the novels that are to be discussed in this chapter, it is useful alongside *Tokyo* to examine the ways in which Hayder is looking to alternative cultures to inject something different into her work. That said, there are *some* Gothic features to this text, and they are indeed worthy of some investigation. One of the most obvious of these is of course the significance of the setting in relation to the nature of the events that take place within the novel. Like many traditional Gothic novels setting, be it a castle or another form of dwelling, has always been intrinsically related to the main theme of the text. The isolation of the final scenes in Shelley's *Frankenstein* captured perfectly the feelings of isolation and loneliness that were such a part of both the monster and Victor Frankenstein's states of mind throughout much of the text and is an excellent example of the way in which location and state of mind can be made to link together for maximum effect. Bristol not only has appropriate context in terms of its historical connection to West Africa and to slavery, but it also permits the development one of the Gothic's strongest themes, that secrets can never remain secrets and that the past will come back to haunt you at some point in time. Bristol has a connection to the exploitation and abuse of African people and this aspect of its history has a strong bearing upon the novel itself, as the particular African culture that is represented in the text is somewhat ironically revenging itself upon the vulnerable of Bristol.

The novel also demonstrates Gothic influence in its detailing of the taking of human body parts for horrific purposes. Although not a part of early Gothic writing, the works of Shelley, Stoker and Polidori all contain elements of dismemberment of some form (and I include blood taking in this) that is echoed throughout Hayder's text. Possession of the human body and the human mind and the way in which this can induce a degree of power for the villain has been a recurrent and strong theme within the

Gothic and it is through the theme of African muti within Hayder's text that the novel has its strongest link to the genre. In the text Mallow's blood is sold to and stored by Kwanele Dlamini in order for Dlamini to engineer some form of protection for himself against the Tokoloshe that he believes to be following him. This is the same sense of self-preservation and survival instinct that governed the way in which Manfred behaved back in *Otranto*. Despite the differing subject matter and context, what ultimately links these two characters is the sense within the Gothic that survival is paramount and that in order to survive the suffering, exploitation and ultimate possession of another human being is required.

Similarly Mallow's hands are removed and sold under the belief that they will bring financial success and prosperity to Mabuza's harbour-side restaurant. Ultimately Mallow's hands are taken as a result of Mabuza's greed and utter disregard for another person's rights and well-being. If we understand the success of his business as being crucial to his survival (as it relates to his financial success), then we can begin to understand how in *this* particular text, like so many traditional Gothic texts, survival becomes paramount and one person's survival is always dependent upon another's suffering. This particularly gory aspect is also reminiscent of the way in which Fuyuki harvested body parts (human organs for the most part) during his time in Nanking. Again this was linked to the desire to survive at any cost. Afflicted by malaria, Fuyuki's desire was to seek for himself a medicine that would cure him; another example of a Gothic villain willing to pursue his own desires with scant regard for those hurt or killed in the process. Certainly a unifying theme within all these Gothic villains has been the unwavering belief that success (in whatever definition of 'success' they hold – it is of course entirely subjective) is an entitlement achievable by whatever means necessary or available to them.

Caffery: Hero or Villain?

Of course in *Ritual* Hayder has re-introduced the character of Jack Caffery and resultingly the novel has significance within the Gothic genre and also the detective genre in a way that *Tokyo* did not. In keeping with many other examples of fictional detectives from modern crime fiction, Caffery is presented, as he has been throughout each of the previous novels that he has featured in (*Birdman* and *The Treatment*), as a veritable mixture of good and bad. He perhaps is more deeply troubled than any other similar detective that we have studied so far, but certainly he follows in the trend of flawed hero that is so much a part of the genre today. He is violent, abusive and incapable of forming relationships. He is only interested in his job in as much as it helps him to atone for the responsibility he feels surrounding the disappearance of his nine-year-old brother, Ewan, when they were children.

In a significant step forward in detailing the personal history of the detective we can see that Caffery is altogether a more complex character. Whereas Rebus was hard drinking, essentially a loner with a failed marriage behind him at least he demonstrated interest in his job for the right reasons. In *Ritual* there are several instances where Caffery's motives behind his chosen profession are indeed questionable. He confesses that he doesn't really 'care'[225] if BM speaks to him or not, and his desire to let his 'debt' to Ewan control his life is not something that is lost on the Walking Man:

> When I said you're looking for death I meant that you've chosen to
> follow the child that's gone. Every step you take in your job, every
> move, is you making gifts to him – to Ewan. Every case you solve is just
> something else to lay at his altar.[226]

Of course there are worse reasons for choosing to become a police officer, and there is nothing really *corrupt* about Caffery, but what his outlook tells us is that he is more in league with the hard-boiled school of detectives, and that what he sees as his 'mission' is less for the good of society for society's sake and more about a personal crusade that just happens to help other victims along the way.

It must not be forgotten however, that Caffery is not the only detective at work within this novel as he is teamed with Sergeant Marley, the police diver who finds the first hand in the harbour. Here Hayder is continuing an ongoing trend within detective fiction for a lead detective to have a 'sidekick' of some sort. Whilst the sidekick doesn't always have to be from law enforcement or have a background in any aspect of policing (Hercule Poirot's Captain Hastings is such an example), it is becoming an increasingly popular tendency within the genre to have pairs of professionals who work in similar fields teaming up. Jeff Tolliver and Sara Linton (Karin Slaughter), Scarpetta and Marino (Cornwell), Brennan and Ryan (Kathy Reichs), Mikael Blomkvist and Lisbeth Salander (Stieg Larsson) are all examples of the way in which teams of different backgrounds can be shown to work together to increase the amount of knowledge and detail within the texts. This technique also offers an alternative perspective. With each new introduction of a 'speciality' another new sub-genre is formed and the genre can continue to avoid the repetition of theme and structure and the autonomy of plot that consumed early Gothic writing.

So what can be made of Sergeant Marley? Again the amount of personal history that we are given is extensive. We know that she has lost both her parents and that she is struggling to manage the upkeep of the family home that she and her brother inherited upon their parents' death. We know also that she finds it difficult to connect fully with her brother and that, like Caffery, she is oppressed and overwhelmed by the weight of the guilt that she feels at having not being there to help her parents or her brother when they needed her. The extent of the guilt that she feels at simply having not been there when they died, and for letting her brother take the dive instead of her, has manifested itself peculiarly in the form of the growth of webbing between her toes. Caffery, too, is equally as affected by the guilt he feels over Ewan (although it does not show itself in such a physical way as Marley's guilt does) and his guilt is evident in the way that he manages to superimpose Penderecki's face onto those that he attacks.

During his struggle with the paedophile outside the supermarket he finds that he can't 'get Penderecki's face out of his head'[227] and whilst listening to the Walking Man's description of his own attack upon the paedophile that killed *his* daughter, Caffery 'replaces Evan's face with the one he wanted in his own fantasy. Ivan Penderecki.'[228] That Caffery and Marley are both so affected and continue to be haunted by the events of their pasts is yet another development of the profile of the detective in modern crime fiction.

Like *Tokyo*, the narrative within *Ritual* is structured so that the novel can shift between the past and the present, and also written from multiple viewpoints to permit us greater insight into a greater number of characters. The novel takes place over five days, and such a huge amount of action takes place over these five days that the pace and suspense of the novel is maintained throughout the text. We, as reader, are given no respite from the frenzied investigation and nor are we spared any of the gruesome details of the crimes themselves.

The Fear of the Unknown

In *Pig Island*, Hayder manages to further manipulate the concept of the 'detective' within modern crime fiction, by this time presenting us with a journalist, Joe Oakes, who will take the primary role in uncovering the 'hoax' and suspicion surrounding the mysterious Pig Island. In this text too

Hayder has chosen a subject matter that in the modern world has a degree of stigma attached to it, that of the cult, and the novel exposes the way in which these are so often misunderstood and feared by those outside of the group.

Written in the first person the novel opens with very little preamble before we are exposed to the main theme of the novel – that of the 'hoax' video of the mysterious creature seen walking the shores of Pig Island. Oakes, it transpires, has been invited to the island by the members of The Psychogenic Healing Ministries themselves in an attempt to quash the rumours of devil worship and bizarre ritualistic behaviour that have dogged the cult since the recording of the video. In terms of setting and location, Pig Island certainly has all the trappings of the typical Gothic setting. Although British, its status as a small, relatively unknown Hebridean island set off the Craignish Peninsula ensures that it has enough mystery surrounding it to alert our suspicions as to the true nature of the goings-on of the island.

Its remoteness and isolation are evident in the way in which access to the island is limited and subject to the weather. Limited access of this sort was certainly a feature that worked exceptionally well in Susan Hill's 1983 novel *The Woman in Black*. In this particular example it is the somewhat sinister Eel Marsh House that forms the primary setting for the location, and the house is only reachable at low tide by crossing the Nine Lives Causeway. The sudden onset of thick fogs, to which the area is prone, also limits access to the house, and it is these fogs that leave Kipps stranded at the house on more than one occasion. Isolation of location is of course a strong feature within Gothic writing, with writers such as Poe, Shelley and Stoker all making use of the greater degree of mystery that can be generated by locating their texts (or at least part of their texts) in areas that are set apart.

The majority of the subject matter of Hayder's text is suitably Gothic too – namely the seeming presence of a half-human half-animal creature that appears to be prowling amongst the woodland along the coastal front of the island. The presence of the beast in combination with the pig remains that regularly get washed ashore along the mainland have led those who live on the mainland to suspect the islanders of belonging to a sinister cult that practises some form of devil worship. Whilst devil worship as such has never been a regular feature of traditional or conventional Gothic writing, the earliest forms of the genre do promote Providence as a reward for goodness over evil and certainly the fact that the islanders seem (through their isolation and reluctance to mingle with the mainland community) to have strayed from God does carry echoes of this early Gothic theme.

Similar to the civilised greeting that the Count offers Jonathan Harker in *Dracula*, the inhabitants of Pig Island are keen to demonstrate their ordinariness to their visitor, and they lavish Joe with food, company and good cheer in an attempt to present him with an image of normality:

> And that was supposed to be the first impression I got – normality
> and sunny wholesomeness through and through, from the gingham
> tablecloth to the homey food…Sunshine in a bottle. That was what they
> wanted me to think.[229]

Just as it failed to put Jonathan Harker's mind at rest in Stoker's text, Oakes similarly refuses to be taken in, recognising it for the 'PR job'[230] that it obviously is and picking up on the tensions that continue to run despite their best intentions at presenting an image of utter happiness and contentment.

Coupled with this Gothic setting and the unease that the location generates, the novel also has a clear sense of typical Gothic characters; there is the villain (Malachi), the victim (Angeline – although her status as victim is questioned at the end of the text as Hayder brings a new dimension to modern crime fiction, that of 'the twist') and the hero (Oakes). Oakes, in keeping with the trend for the 'detective' within modern crime fiction is flawed and in the midst of battling personal demons (a failing marriage in this example). He is invited to Pig Island by the islanders in order that he can write an article about the good work that they do on the island and to dispel the rumour that they are devil-worshippers.

It is a summons that Oakes is sceptical about, referring to the islanders before he has even met them, as 'nutsos' and as people who can 'get by on green tea and glasses of their own urine'[231]. It is not long however before he realises exactly how wrong he is and begins to understand how they live in fear of their deranged ex-leader, Malachi Dove. (The extent of their fear is revealed by Sovereign as she explains the need for bolts on the church doors, 'How stupid are you? Not out! *In*. They're not trying to stop anyone getting *out*. They're trying to stop something getting *in*.'[232]) Because the islanders live in such constant fear of Dove it is easy to see how the islanders also take on the role of Gothic victim(s). They are oppressed and live in fear of something that they do not understand (the presence of the 'biforme'[233] that they believe Dove to have conjured) and to this extent are suffering.

Throughout the novel the real victim is presumed to be Dove's daughter, Angeline, the child that Dove had everyone believe to have been stillborn. It is not until the second half of the novel, and the action moves away from Pig Island that we realise the true extent of the abuse that Angeline has suffered at the hands of her father. In taking her away from Dove, however, Oakes manages only to substitute one villain for another, and Dove's villainy is soon replaced by exploitation and abuse from Oakes' wife, Lexie. It is in the latter half of the novel that Hayder introduces Lexie as a narrator, and from this point onwards we are able to witness the story as it unfolds from the point of view of both Oakes and his wife. Being able to write so effectively from multiple viewpoints is something that Hayder does extremely well. Certainly without it we would not have such an opportunity to 'get inside' the minds of the central characters in the way that is such a common feature within modern crime fiction. The fact that we are allowed to witness innermost thoughts first hand in this way shows just how extensively the Gothic genre has changed over the years, in that now we are allowed direct access to our characters thoughts and feeling. In the original form of the genre such access was only gained through metaphorical allusion to a particular home or castle or through the use of pathetic fallacy to signify the onset of a breakdown through ominous weather or similar. The advent of first-person narrative, multiple narrators and shifting tenses has allowed for greater complexity of character and plot than was seen in either early Gothic or early detective fiction, and they are each a strong identifier of modern crime fiction.

The Introduction of 'The Twist'

Clearly Hayder has made advancements within the genre, most notably with regards to the introduction of the concept of 'the twist' as is evident at the end of *Pig Island*. Within detective fiction *itself* the concept of a red herring, false clue or a twist is not a new feature, but until this point it has been relatively unexploited in modern crime fiction. If we are to accept modern crime fiction as being comprised of the Gothic *and* detective fiction, then the way in which Angeline Dove is revealed to have set Oakes up is clearly one of the strongest links to the detective aspect of the genre's origins. The way in which Oakes (as the novel's 'detective') remains ignorant of Angeline's true character until the end of the novel is quite clearly linked to the propensity within modern crime fiction for people or places to secrete sinister aspects within them and to simultaneously act as hero *and* villain. That we do not see Angeline coming allows for a greater degree of shock for the reader and incorporates a greater degree of cunning, premeditation and sophistication on the part of the writer than was ever evident in early Gothic or early detective fiction. In combining these two genres, Hayder's modern crime fiction extracts the best features of each, manipulating them to produce a new perspective and direction that prevent rigidity and predictability within the narrative.

Hayder also makes significant changes to the anticipated narrative structure of the modern crime novel. Multiple viewpoints and the constant shift between the past and the present in a great many of her texts add a great degree of complexity to the writing and permit readers to gain greater proximity to more than one character within the text in a more insightful way than hearing of events past through letter or diary entry. There is also a significant shift in the degree to which conventional Gothic form or theme is relied upon, or exploited, within her texts. Whereas in so many of the examples of modern crime fiction explored so far in this book, heavy reliance upon Gothic form has helped to maintain the tradition of conveying social context within the main plot of the story, Hayder chooses not to do this and consequently she is the author who demonstrates perhaps the least evidence of the Gothic being such a important and recognisable part of her work.

It is indeed a new direction for the genre that brings with it a degree of refreshing change. Gothicised modern crime fiction is a popular genre and severely at risk of becoming just as rigid in structure and form as early Gothic writing became. To become so conventional in form is something that will inevitably draw parody in the future and the genre will begin to lose integrity. By offering this new alternative Hayder is indeed looking for a means by which to avoid this, and the result is not only a new direction for the genre, but also a more interesting reading experience as we are encouraged to re-think the way we approach the genre. It is interesting to see the way in which the genre can operate away from its Gothic roots and reassuring to see that a concept of the 'story' is not compromised in any way by this departure from Gothic form. Nothing is lost from the plot, the narrative or the enjoyment that we derive from reading one of Hayder's texts. In a genre that already has numerous sub-genres and complex classifications Hayder has managed to find room for something new and what this demonstrates is that there is still scope within the genre in which to be experimental and to try new things.

Where the genre goes from here is of course anyone's guess; writers are always looking to push boundaries and to manipulate existing form – wanting to put as much of their own stamp upon the literary world as best they can. In studying the origins of the Gothic genre, the move into detective fiction and the emergence of modern crime fiction (including examples of some of the most recent modern crime fiction to be published) there is only one thing left to do within this text, and that is to pull together the key strands that will tell us exactly how much of a Gothic footprint (if any) is left in today's modern crime fiction.

CHAPTER EIGHT

Drawing Conclusions: Understanding Modern Crime Fiction

G ENRE classification is a complex thing and underneath the enormous umbrella of classified works of fiction, there are many ways in which a novel might be categorised. Most of us are probably familiar with the act of browsing for books under shelves labelled science fiction, horror, crime or romance for example, depending upon where our interests lie, but there are problems associated with trying to give definitive labels to fictional texts. Increasingly texts are becoming more multilayered, operating on a number of different levels and with a range of plots and subplots that make classification of the novel within traditional guidelines a very difficult thing to do.

Essentially following and charting the development and growth of modern crime fiction, specifically the way in which it has grown out of the Gothic has been the main focus of this text. In picking apart the 'bare bones' of the Gothic and understanding the rigidity of its form it is possible to see that there is more than just a hint of the Gothic evident in much of the modern crime fiction that has been studied within this text. It is not enough, however, simply to categorise modern crime fiction as a modern re-hash of the old Gothic form and label it as such. Understanding the genre in its entirety is more complex than that and must also take into account the influence that detective fiction has upon it. The suggestion that detective fiction emerged from the Gothic has already been made in Chapter 2 of this book, and following this it has been argued that at its most basic definition, modern crime fiction is a result of a fusion between the Gothic and detective fiction.

Modern Crime Fiction: The Rise of a Genre

In examples of early Modern crime fiction it is easy to understand how this fusion works; in Bloch's *Psycho* there is a clear sense of the Gothic at work and also a clear detective-based theme present within the text. With the exception of Norman's complex psychological issues, the novel is relatively simple in its execution; the number of characters are relatively few and it is easy to identify the standard Gothic 'type' on which they are based. The novel is also very linear in its progression – moving from beginning to end with no movement between tenses or time frames.

However, the fact that the novel is relatively 'simple' in concept and form should not be considered detrimental in any way to the overall *success* of the novel, and part of its charm and effect is *due to* and *because* of its simplicity. It is only when compared to the most recent examples of modern crime fiction, and Hayder is an excellent example of up–to-the-minute modern crime fiction, that we are able to look back and understand the growth in the genre's complexity. *Psycho* is a novel that is heavily influenced by a number of different Gothic conventions, and owes a great deal to the Gothic form it terms of its success. Were the Gothic elements to be removed from the narrative then quite simply the novel would be altered to such an extent that the entire aspect of the story would waver. The novel would cease to be a modern crime fiction text and would exist solely as a detective novel instead. Indeed we can say the same for almost every example of modern crime fiction studied hereto; that were the Gothic trace be removed, the character of each of the novels would alter so significantly that they would no longer operate as successful examples of modern crime fiction. Certainly this can be seen to great extent in the novels of Patricia Cornwell, specifically *Black Notice*, as so many aspects of this novel (plot, character, setting and narrative viewpoint) are heavily influenced by Gothic form and to remove them would see the face of the text changed irrecoverably and much of its lost. Essentially it would become a simple murder story, the villains of which would become nothing more than a pair of psychotic brothers rampaging across America, with no subtext, alternative meaning or contextual implication.

It is only when the development of modern crime fiction is chronologically analysed in this way that the degree to which Gothic form is still influencing the genre becomes apparent, and it is only in recent years that the genre has shown any signs of possessing the ability to break away from the Gothic and to emerge as an entirely separate form of writing. In many ways the earliest form of modern crime fiction behaved in a similar fashion to the earliest form of detective fiction, and that was to cling to its generic roots before being able to operate successfully and separately from the Gothic. Of course, recognising Gothic influence is the easiest part of understanding modern crime fiction; much harder is attempting to explain *why* the Gothic is such an important part of the genre.

The Allure of the Gothic

Understanding the Gothic is no easy task, and understanding the way in which it continues to influence the creative direction of so many different genres is no mean feat either. Why should it be that so many writers and genres are indebted to the Gothic before developing foundations sufficient enough to move on from the Gothic and leave it behind so to speak?

It has already been pointed out that any 'new' genre that has to do with fear of some sort will find an appropriate host within the Gothic, such is the degree to which the genre deals with issues of fear, unease and uncertainty. But it is not enough to simply state that anything that has to do with fear is inherently Gothic. Because of the propensity within the Gothic to make social observations and carry cultural and contextual relevance it could be argued that any novel wishing to make similar observations about the period in which *it* has been written would find natural affinity with the conventions of early Gothic form; but again this seems an inadequate explanation to *fully* comprehend the allure of the Gothic. This said it would be wrong to dismiss *altogether* the significance and relevance of cultural preoccupation in accounting for the rise of modern crime fiction. After all the novels essentially are about crime, and what is crime if not a measure of society? But the point I make here is that cultural context alone is not sufficient to explain fully the enduring popularity and longevity (irrespective of the adaptations that have occurred over time) of the Gothic genre in all its forms.

Carl Jung: Theories of Archetype

Perhaps the answer to the allure of the Gothic lies in a much more fundamental understanding of the way in which our subconscious and conscious minds respond to the element of pattern, or archetype, with which the Gothic presents us. It is a theory that is worthy of some consideration if we are truly to attempt to get a handle on exactly what it is about the Gothic that has enthralled us and kept us reading Gothic stories for more than 200 years.

First appearing in around 1920, Jung's theories of archetype identify the human need for a degree of routine and predictability in all aspects of life, and given the reading public's affinity with the concept of genre we can safely assume that this that this need for predictability extends to the telling and reading of stories also. If we accept that stories are a 'product of a controlling power that is set in the subconscious' and that 'the very fact that they follow such identifiable patterns and are shaped by such consistent rules indicates that the unconscious is using them for a purpose'[234] then we can begin to see just how Jung's theories may begin to be applied. It is certainly an interesting concept and one that is very relevant to understanding the way in which we are attracted to the Gothic form. In the Gothic we are presented with a degree of autonomy that is clearly linked to our need as humans to have our conscious and subconscious selves presented with archetypal figures and ideas by which we can be simultaneously challenged and reassured. The representation of archetypal 'good' and 'evil' within the Gothic plot ceases to be simply a feature of the narrative and begins to engage with issues that we confront on a daily basis in our conscious lives, and in this respect the restorative power of the Gothic, and the quashing of evil as it occurs in modern crime fiction, cannot be underestimated. The Gothic plays with our fears, expectations and pleasures and confronting each of these aspects is a crucial part of how we begin to understand ourselves and the way in which we interact with those around us and the world as a whole. It has a natural affinity with that which we confront every day and has resultingly become, to varying degrees, a recurrent theme in almost all types of fiction.

Looking to the Future

Certainly we are unlikely to see a revival of the Gothic in its purist form – that which was identified back in Chapter 1 as 'First Phase Gothic' – at any point in the future. The genre is far too diffused and complex to facilitate such a return to the relatively simple structure and motif by which that these first phase texts are characterised. Gothic presence is indeed felt in a number of different genres (detective fiction, romance fiction, science fiction to name but a few) but it is the way in which it is traceable in modern crime fiction that has been the central preoccupation of this book.

That early examples of modern crime fiction posses Gothic influence is undeniable, as is the assertion that early texts rely upon Gothic form as a means of generating both effect and meaning. What is negligible *now* is the extent to which the genre as it stands today remains reliant upon this heavy Gothic influence. Current writers of modern crime fiction (which includes the sub-genres of forensic crime fiction, serial killer fiction among others) are indeed demonstrating increasing ability to reject those aspects of the Gothic that featured so heavily in earlier texts and managing to steer the genre away from its Gothic roots. This text made reference to the work of Mo Hayder as a means of demonstrating this new direction for modern crime fiction, but Hayder is by no means the only current writer able to do this. Both Kathy Reichs and Karin Slaughter have managed to produce a number of texts that function independently from the Gothic and even more recently Stieg Larsson's Millennium Trilogy has demonstrated just how effective a genre modern crime fiction can be in its own right. That each of these novels has remained successful despite the absence of the Gothic from the narrative, almost certainly means that now that the gates have opened to this Gothic-free form of the genre many more writers will follow suit.

That is not to say however, that the Gothic will not appear in some form within another genre at any point in the future; almost without doubt it will. The exciting question is where and when this will occur, and what new genre will emerge? Increasingly the Gothic has become a conduit through which new genres take shape and emerge slowly over a number of years, and whilst this may appear to some as tantamount to exploitation, for me it is tantalising and exciting to wait for the next re-emergence of the Gothic, indicative as it will be of the beginning and development of yet another new genre of writing.

Chronology of Significant Texts

Walpole, Horace. *The Castle of Otranto* (1764)

Burke, Edmund. *Reflections on the Revolution in France* (1790)

Lewis, Matthew. *The Monk* (1796)

Radcliffe, Ann. *The Italian* (1797)

Shelley, Mary. *Frankenstein* (1818)

Polidori, John. *The Vampyre* (1819)

Hawthorne, Nathaniel. *The White Old Maid* (1835)

Poe, Edgar Allan. *The Fall of the House of Usher* (1839)

Poe, Edgar Allan. *The Murders in the Rue Morgue* (1841) – C. Auguste Dupin debuts

Poe, Edgar Allan. *The Mystery of Marie Rogêt* (1842)

Poe, Edgar Allan. *The Tell-Tale Heart* (1843)

Poe, Edgar Allan. *The Black Cat* (1843)

Poe, Edgar Allan. *The Purloined Letter* (1845)

Poe, Edgar Allan. *The Philosophy of Composition* (1846)

Poe, Edgar Allan. *The Cask of Amontillado* (1846)

Hawthorne, Nathaniel. *The House of the Seven Gables* (1851)

Collins, Wilkie. *The Moonstone* (1868)

Stevenson, Robert Louis. *The Strange Case of Dr Jekyll and My Hyde* (1886)

Conan Doyle, Arthur. *A Study in Scarlet* (1887) – Sherlock Holmes debuts

Stoker, Bram. *Dracula* (1897)

Christie, Agatha. *The Mysterious Affair at Styles* (1920) – Hercule Poirot debuts

Christie, Agatha. *The Tuesday Night Club* (1927) – Miss Marple debuts

Hammett, Dashiell. *The Maltese Falcon* (1930) – Sam Spade debuts

Chandler, Raymond. *The Big Sleep* (1939) – Philip Marlowe debuts

Bloch, Robert. *Psycho* (1959)

James, P. D. *Cover Her Face* (1962) – Commander Adam Dalgleish debuts

Rendell, Ruth. *From Doon with Death* (1964) – Chief Inspector Wexford debuts

Dexter, Colin. *Last Bus to Woodstock* (1975) – Inspector Morse debuts

Harris, Thomas. *Red Dragon* (1981) – Dr Hannibal Lecter debuts

Rankin, Ian. *Knots and Crosses* (1987) – Detective Inspector Rebus debuts
Harris, Thomas. *The Silence of the Lambs* (1988)
Cornwell, Patricia. *Postmortem* (1990) – Dr Kay Scarpetta debuts
Welsh, Irvine. *Trainspotting* (1993)
Hayder, Mo. *Birdman* (2000) – Detective Inspector Jack Caffery debuts
Larsson, Stieg. *The Girl with the Dragon Tattoo* – Mikael Blomkvist debuts

Suggested Further Reading

Bloom, Clive. *Gothic Histories: The Taste for Terror – 1764 to the Present* (London: Continuum, 2010)

Booker, Christopher. *The Seven Basic Plots: Why We Tell Stories* (London: Continuum, 2004)

Botting, Fred. *Gothic* (London: Routledge, 2003)

Ellis, Markman. *The History of Gothic Fiction* (Edinburgh: Edinburgh University Press, 2007)

Flanders, Judith. *The Invention of Murder* (London: HarperPress, 2011)

Garland, Rosemary (ed.) *Freakery: Cultural spectacles of the Extraordinary Body* (New York: New York University Press, 1996)

Gregoriou, Christiana. *Deviance in Contemporary Crime Fiction* (Hampshire: Palgrave Macmillan, 2009)

Hamilton Lytle, Mark. *America's Uncivil Wars – The 1960s era from Elvis to the fall of Richard Nixon* (New York: Oxford University Press, 2006)

Kristeva, Julia. *Powers of Horror – An Essay on Abjection* (New York: Columbia University Press, 1982)

Punter, David. *The Literature of Terror Volume 1*(Essex: Longman, 1996)

Sharp, Michael. D. *Popular Contemporary Writers* (New York: Michael Cavendish, 2006)

Simpson, Philip. *Psychopaths: Tracking the Serial Killer Through Contemporary American Film and Fiction* (USA: Southern Illinois University Press, 2000)

Truslow Adams, James. *The Epic of America* (London: Simon Publications, 2001)

Notes

1   Botting, F. *Gothic* (London: Routledge, 2003) p.44.
2   Bloom, C. *Gothic Histories: The Taste for Terror – 1764 TO THE PRESENT* (London: Continuum, 2010) p.2.
3   Punter, D. *The Literature of Terror Volume 1*(Essex: Longman, 1996) p.3.
4   Grey, T. (1751) *Elegy Written in a Country Church-Yard* <http://www.blupete.com/Literature/Poetry/Elegy.htm> accessed 2 January 2010 p.1.
5   Punter, op. cit., pp.9–10.
6   Walpole, H. *The Castle of Otranto* (Oxford: Oxford University Press, 1998) p.109.
7   Reeve, C. *The Old English Baron* in Spector, R. (ed.) *Seven Masterpieces of Gothic Horror* (New York: Bantam Books, 1970) p.105.
8   Ibid., p.147.
9   Botting, op. cit., p.44.
10 Stevens, D. *The Gothic Tradition* (Cambridge: Cambridge University Press, 2004) p.46.
11 Botting, op. cit., p.45.
12 Punter, op. cit., p.1.
13 Austen, J. *Northanger Abbey* (London: Penguin, 1995) p.143.
14 Ellis, M. *The History of Gothic Fiction* (Edinburgh: Edinburgh University Press, 2007) p.81.
15 Ibid., p.81.
16 Ibid., p.81.
17 Burke, E. (1790) *Reflections on the Revolution in France* <http://www.constitution.org/eb/rev_fran.htm> accessed 29 June 2010. p.4.
18 Ibid., p.3.
19 Ibid., p.4.
20 Ellis, op. cit., p.81.
21 Lewis, M. *The Monk* (Oxford: Oxford, 1980) p.vii.
22 Ibid., p.xii.
23 Ibid., p.xii.
24 Tooley, B. (2000) *Gothic Utopia: Heretical Sanctuary in Ann Radcliffe's Italian*, <http://findarticles.com/p/articles/mi_7051/is_2_11/ai_n28819166/> accessed 5 November 2008. p.1.
25 Ibid., p.1.
26 Punter, op. cit., p.82.
27 Shelley, Mary: *Frankenstein* (London: Penguin, 1992) pp.99–100.
28 Ibid., p.xix.
29 Ibid., p.xix.
30 Ibid., p.xxiv.
31 Ibid., p.215.
32 Ibid., p.215.
33 Ibid., p.215.
34 Polidori, J. *The Vampyre* (Oxford: Oxford University Press, 1998) p.3.
35 Shelley, op. cit., p.56.
36 Beckford, W. *Vathek* (Oxford: Oxford University Press, 1998) p.1.
37 Bloom, op. cit., p.80.
38 Le Fanu, S. *Carmilla* in Spector, R. (ed.) *Seven Masterpieces of Gothic*

Horror (New York: Bantam Books, 1970) p.398.

39 Stoker, B. *Dracula* (London: Penguin, 1993) pp.19–23.

40 Polidori, op.cit., p.xix.

41 Ibid., p.xix.

42 Spector (ed.), op. cit., p.396.

43 Ibid., p.396

44 Stoker, op. cit., p.xxiv.

45 Ibid., p.ix.

46 Botting, op. cit., p.136.

47 Ibid., p.156.

48 Ibid., p.157.

49 Ibid., p.157.

50 Matheson, R. *I am Legend* (London: Orion Books, 2007) p.18.

51 Stevens, op. cit., p.31.

52 Bloom, op. cit p.62.

53 Hawthorne, N. *The House of the Seven Gables* (New York: Bantam Books, 1981). p.1.

54 Cunningham, A. *The Master of Logan* (1831). In Morrison, R. and Baldick, C. (eds) *John Polidori: The Vampyre and Other Tales of the Macabre* (Oxford: Oxford University Press, 1998) p.63.

55 Hawthorne, op. cit., p.5.

56 Miller, R. *MYSTERY! Case Book: Old Dark Houses*, <http://www.pbs.org/wgbh/mystery/essays/darkhouses.html> accessed 9th March 2011. p.2.

57 Punter, op. cit., pp.173–5.

58 Botting, op. cit., p.115.

59 Galloway, D. In *The Fall of the House of Usher And Other Writings* (London: Penguin Books, 1986) p.43.

60 Hawthorne, N. *The White Old Maid* in Spector, R. (ed.) *Seven Masterpieces of Gothic Horror* (New York: Bantam Books, 1970) p.365.

61 Poe, E A. *The Cask of Amontillado*. In Symons, J. ed., *Edgar Allan Poe Selected Tales*. (Oxford, Oxford University Press, 1980) p.278.

62 Poe, E A. *The Tell-Tale Heart*. In Symons, J. ed., *Edgar Allan Poe*

63 *Selected Tales.* (Oxford, Oxford University Press, 1980) p.186.

63 Ibid., p.186.

64 Ibid., p.186.

65 Poe, E A. *The Black Cat.* In Symons, J. ed., *Edgar Allan Poe Selected Tales*. (Oxford, Oxford University Press, 1980) p.193.

66 Ibid., p.193.

67 Giddings, R. *Poe: Rituals of Life and Death.* In Docherty, B. ed., *American Horror Fiction: From Brockden Brown to Stephen King.* (London: Macmillan, 1990.) p.46.

68 Ibid., p.46–7.

69 Poe, *The Tell-Tale Heart* op. cit., p.188.

70 Poe, *The Black Cat* op. cit., p.197.

71 Ibid., p.198.

72 Giddings, op. cit., p.47.

73 Ibid., p.47.

74 Cheney, M. *Chronicles of the Damned: The crimes and punishments of the condemned felons of Newgate Gaol* (Somerset: Marston House, 1992) p.83.

75 Poe, E A. *The Murders in the Rue Morgue.* In Symons, J. ed., *Edgar Allan Poe Selected Tales.* (Oxford, Oxford University Press, 1980) p.108.

76 Marling, W. (25th June 2007) *Detective Novels: An Overview*, <http://www.detnovel.com/> accessed 5th October 2009. p.1.

77 Ibid., p.1.

78 Poe, E A. *The Purloined Letter.* In Symons, J. ed., *Edgar Allan Poe Selected Tales.* (Oxford, Oxford University Press, 1980) p.213.

79 Poe, E. A. (1846)*The Philosophy of Composition*, <http://www.poeticbyway.com/philo.htm> p.1. accessed 20th July 2010.

80 Ibid., p.2.

81 Collins, W. *The Moonstone* (London: Penguin, 1986) p.16.

82 Allingham, P. (14th November 2000) *Dickens' "Hunted Down"*

(1859): A First Person Narrative of Poisoning and Life-Insurance Fraud Influenced by Wilkie Collins, <http://www.victorianweb.org/authors/dickens/pva/pva19.html> accessed 25ᵗʰ January 2011. p.1.

83 Eagleton, T. In Dickens, C *Bleak House* (London: Penguin, 2003) p.vi.

84 Ibid., p.x.

85 Ibid., p.x.

86 Conan Doyle, A. *The Hound of the Baskervilles* in *The Hound of the Baskervilles & The Valley of Fear* (Herefordshire: Wordsworth Classics,1999) p.162.

87 Ibid., p.19.

88 Ibid p.57.

89 Bargainnier, Earl. F. *The Gentle Art of Murder: The Detective Fiction of Agatha Christie*, (Ohio: Bowling Green University Popular Press, 1980) p.10.

90 Ibid., p.10.

91 Ibid., p.10.

92 Ibid., p.10.

93 Knox, R. (1929) *10 Commandments of Detective Fiction*, <http://www.writingclasses.com/InformationPages/index.php/PageID/303> p.1. accessed 6ᵗʰ August 2010.

94 Horsley, L. *American Hard-Boiled Crime Fiction, 1920s-1940s*, <http://www.crimeculture.com/Contents/Hard-Boiled.html> p.1. accessed 3ʳᵈ August 2010

95 Ousby, I. *Guilty Parties: A Mystery Lover's Companion*, (New York: Thames and Hudson, 1997.) p.92.

96 Ibid., pp.92–3.

97 Punter, D. 'Robert Bloch's *Psycho*: Some Pathological Contexts'. In *American Horror Fiction: From Brockden Brown to Stephen King* (Hampshire: Macmillan Press, 2002) p.92.

98 Bloch, R. *Psycho* (London: Corgi Books, 1969) p.110.

99 Ibid., p.7.

100 Dickens, C. *Great Expectations*, <http://www.dickens-literature.com/Great_Expectations/0.html> accessed 8ᵗʰ September 2010. p.1.

101 Bloch, op. cit., p.117.

102 Poe, E. *The Fall of the House of Usher* in Galloway, D. ed., *The Fall of the House of Usher and Other Writings* (London: Penguin Books, 1986) p.149.

103 Bloch, op. cit., p.26.

104 Ibid., p.27.

105 See Punter, op. cit., p.94.

106 Stevenson, R. *The Strange Case of Dr Jekyll and Mr Hyde* (London: Penguin Books, 1994) p.70.

107 Ibid., p.71.

108 Ibid., p.29.

109 Ibid., p.30.

110 Ibid., p.23.

111 Bloch, op. cit., p.21.

112 Ibid., p.21.

113 Ibid., p.118.

114 Hamilton Lytle, M. *America's Uncivil Wars – The 1960s era from Elvis to the fall of Richard Nixon* (Oxford University Press: New York, 2006) p.x.

115 Ibid., p.xiii.

116 Simpson, P. *Psychopaths: Tracking the Serial Killer Through Contemporary American Film and Fiction* (Southern Illinois University Press: USA, 2000) p.2.

117 Ibid., p.70.

118 Ibid., p.84.

119 Harris, T. *Red Dragon* (Peerage Books: London, 1991) p.177.

120 Ibid., p.53.

121 Ibid., Title Page.

122 Ibid., p.12.

123 Ibid., p.7.

124 Simpson, op. cit., p.72.

125 Hamilton Lytle, op. cit., p.2.

126 Hamilton Lytle, M. *America's Uncivil Wars – The Sixties Era From Elvis To The Fall of Richard Nixon*

(Oxford University Press: New York, 2006) p.1.

127 Harris, op. cit., p.74.

128 Harris, T. *The Silence of the Lambs* (Peerage Books: London, 1991) p.390.

129 Harris, *Dragon* op. cit., p.75.

130 (4th July 1776) *The American Declaration of Independence* <http://www.ushistory.org/declaration/document> accessed 27th September 2010. p.1.

131 Harris, T. *Hannibal* (Arrow Books: London, 2000) p.418.

132 Harris, *Silence* op. cit., p.289.

133 Ibid., p.295.

134 Ibid., p.295.

135 Harris, *Hannibal* op. cit., p.37.

136 Harris, *Silence* op. cit., p.339.

137 Ibid., p.350.

138 Harris, *Dragon* op. cit., p.17.

139 Ibid., p.24.

140 Ibid., p.24.

141 Ibid., p.54.

142 Ibid., pp.117–8.

143 Ibid., p.135.

144 Ibid., p.25.

145 Harris, *Silence* op. cit., p.324.

146 Harris, *Hannibal* op. cit., p.55.

147 Ibid., p.299.

148 Simpson, op. cit., p.76.

149 Ibid., p.78.

150 Ibid., p.78.

151 Harris, *Silence* op. cit., p.299.

152 Ibid., p.299.

153 Harris, *Hannibal* op. cit., p.4.

154 Ibid., p.4.

155 Ibid., p.6.

156 Maslin, J. (11th December 2006) *Book Review – Hannibal Rising* <http://www.nytimes.com/2006/12/11/arts/11iht-bookmar.3854002.html> accessed 12th October 2010. p.1.

157 Poole, S. (16th December 2006) *Portrait of the monster as a young boy* <http://www.guardian.co.uk./books/2006/dec/16/fiction.

thomasharris> accessed 12th October 2010 p.1.

158 Harris, *Hannibal* op. cit., p.554.

159 Rankin, I. *Knots and Crosses* (Orion Books: London, 2005) p.7.

160 Rankin, I. *The Naming of the Dead* (Orion Books: London, 2007) pp.44–5.

161 Rankin, I. *The Falls* (Orion Books: London, 2001) p.153.

162 Rankin, I. *Mortal Causes* (Orion Books: London, 2008) p.20.

163 Rankin, *The Naming of the Dead* op. cit., pp.101–2.

164 Rankin, I. *Fleshmarket Close* (Orion Books: London, 2005) p.6.

165 Ibid., p. 472.

166 Rankin, I. *Doors Open* (Orion Books: London, 2008) p.205.

167 Rankin, *The Naming of the Dead* op. cit., p.29.

168 Rankin, *Fleshmarket* op. cit., p.18.

169 Rankin, I. *Dead Souls* (Orion Books: London, 2008) p.464.

170 Rankin, *The Falls* op. cit., p.97.

171 Rankin, *Mortal* op. cit., p.3.

172 Ibid., p.304.

173 Rankin, *Dead Souls* op. cit., p.481.

174 Rankin, *Mortal* op. cit., pp.1–2.

175 Rankin, *Dead Souls* op. cit., p.450.

176 Rendell, R. *Simisola* (Arrow Books: London, 1995) pp.209–10.

177 Rankin, *Fleshmarket* op. cit., p.6.

178 Simpson, op. cit., p.114.

179 Sharp, M. D. *Popular Contemporary Writers* (Michael Cavendish: New York, 2006) p.491.

180 Ibid., p.483.

181 Gregoriou, C. *Deviance in Contemporary Crime Fiction* (Palgrave Macmillan: Hampshire, 2009) p.111.

182 Ibid., p.111.

183 Garland, R (ed.) *Freakery: Cultural spectacles of the Extraordinary Body* (New York University Press: New York, 1996) p.xiii.

184 Ibid., p.xiii.

185 Ibid., p.1.

186 Cornwell, P. *Blow Fly* (Time Warner Paperbacks: London, 2003) p.68.
187 Cornwell, P. *Black Notice* (Time Warner Books: London, 2006) p.324.
188 Cornwell, P. *The Last Precinct* (Time Warner Books: London, 2006) p.174.
189 Ibid., p.67.
190 Hugo, V. *Notre-Dame de Paris* (Oxford World's Classics: New York: 2009) p.155.
191 Ibid., p.154.
192 Cornwell, *Black Notice* op. cit., p.376.
193 Cornwell, *The Last Precinct* op. cit., p.174.
194 Ibid., p.6.
195 Ibid., p.101.
196 Frostchild, D. (September 1999) *Werewolves and Dysfunctional Families: Another Mixed Bag from Patricia Cornwell*, <http://www,thewag.net/books/cornwell.htm> accessed 24th February 2009.p.4.
197 Cornwell, *Blow Fly* op. cit., p. 364.
198 Ibid., p.365.
199 Cornwell, *Black Notice* op. cit., p.380.
200 Cornwell, *Blow Fly* op. cit., p.305.
201 Cornwell, *Black Notice* op. cit., p.402.
202 Ibid., p.316.
203 Cornwell, *The Last Precinct* op. cit., p.258.
204 Ibid., p.77.
205 Cornwell, *Blow Fly* op. cit., p.12.
206 Ibid., p.138
207 Ibid., p.138.
208 Ibid., p.20.
209 Ibid., p.20.
210 Simpson, *Psychopaths* op. cit., p.115.
211 Ibid., p.521.
212 Cornwell, *The Last Precinct* op. cit., p.111.
213 Ibid., p.113.
214 Cornwell, *Black Notice* op. cit. P.293.
215 Cornwell, *The Last Precinct* op. cit., p.274.
216 Ibid., p.211.
217 Ibid., p.303.
218 Cornwell, *Blow Fly* op. cit., p.106–7.
219 Ibid., p.395.
220 Cornwell, *The Last Precinct* op. cit., p.88.
221 Hayder, M. *Tokyo* (Bantam Books: London, 2004) p.53.
222 Ibid., p.123.
223 High, C. *Interview with Mo Hayder*, <http://www.chrishigh.com/interviews/mo_hayder_interview_2007.htm> accessed 4th November 2010. p.2.
224 Hayder, M. *Ritual* (Bantam Books: London, 2008) pp426–30.
225 Ibid., p.172.
226 Ibid., p.538.
227 Ibid., p.487.
228 Ibid., p.357.
229 Hayder, M. *Pig Island* (Bantam Books: London, 2006) p.63.
230 Ibid., p.63.
231 Ibid., pp.48–9.
232 Ibid., p.78.
233 Ibid., p.105.
234 Booker, C. *The Seven Basic Plots: Why We Tell Stories* (Continuum: London, 2004) p.553.

Index